1500 *days*

OF FUN THINGS TO DO IN

RETIREMENT

DANIEL DAVIDS

2

"There Is A Fountain Of Youth:
It Is Your Mind, Your Talents,
The Creativity You Bring To Your Life
And The Lives Of People You Love.
When You Learn To Tap This Source,
You Will Truly Have Defeated Age."

-Sophia Loren-

A SPECIAL REQUEST

I REALLY APPRECIATE YOUR SUPPORT!
A SHORT, SIMPLE REVIEW ON THE AMAZON PAGE
WILL BE VERY HELPFULL FOR ME.

THANK YOU
FOR CHOOSING
MY BOOK!

DANIEL DAVIDS

TABLE OF CONTENTS

INTRODUCTION

"DANCE, LIVE, SING, CRY, LOVE, TRAVEL AND LOVE AGAIN,
UNTIL THE DAY YOU HAVE TO STOP."
-VANESSA VANNY THOMPSON-

Depending on what you decide to do in retirement, leaving the workforce might be an opportunity to rediscover your deepest passions and most significant objectives. You can experiment with new things, learn, and spend more time with the people and activities you enjoy. Of course, all of it is up to you.

When you retire, you are liberated from the pressure of meeting work-related deadlines and can enjoy your free time however you like. You can also benefit from a wide range of senior discounts, even though your income may be lower than it was while you were working full-time, and you might not have any debts like a mortgage, student loans, or credit card debt. According to a Merrill Lynch survey, retirement is the moment in people's adult lives when they feel the happiest, most at ease, and least anxious.

Leisure during a person's working years frequently entails unwinding and getting away from routine. But in retirement, it's more important to be active and socialize. So to keep you physically active, mentally challenged, and actively involved in possibilities for sociability and enjoyment, I've found a wide range of activities.

But keep in mind that retirement is all about freedom and choice. Use these ideas as inspiration to forge your own course; they are merely a starting point.

TRAVEL THE WORLD

"Go at Least Once a Year to a Place
You've Never Been Before."
-Dalai Lama-

Fulfill your wanderlust! With no restrictions on your vacation time, you can travel the world. Retirees have the freedom to take extended vacations and take advantage of last-minute deals. Many people enjoy taking regular trips to go biking, golfing, shopping, or to the arts. Some stay close to home, while others travel further afield to places like the Caribbean, Europe, and Latin America.

Consider the following senior travel suggestions:

MINI-TOUR OF COSTA RICAN CULTURE FOR 12 DAYS

Costa Rica is the place to live your Pura Vida! This breathtaking Central American country is ideal for anyone looking for a relaxing vacation. Costa Rica has it all: turquoise waters, treetop zip lines, delicious fruit, and sloths. Learn about the beautiful culture and rich history of the world's happiest place! Worldaway Learning Tours provides an all-inclusive trip that includes lodging, three meals per day, expert local guides, and a variety of immersive activities and excursions. Visit the UNESCO World Heritage Site of the Diquis Stone Spheres. Visit Providencia, a rural community known for its giant oak trees, coffee plantations, and birdwatching. And don't forget to try some fresh cacao hot chocolate!

CYCLING THROUGH THE NETHERLANDS: TULIPS AND WINDMILLS

Bicycle through Holland's famed tulip fields while learning about the country's windmills, diving into the flower industry and taking in the world-famous Bloemencorso flower parade.

ATHENS, MYKONOS, AND SANTORINI IN ONE WEEK

From the hilltops of Greece's most famous islands, watch the sunset. The picturesque Greek landscapes include cobblestone streets, arched white facades, ocean-blue roofs, and larger-than-life windmills. In Athens, you can learn about ancient history and visit open-air museums. Then, on the isles of Mykonos and Santorini, the quintessential, beautiful Greek islands you've been dreaming of coming to life.

NORTH CAROLINA, AGATHA CHRISTIE, CLASSIC FILM MYSTERIES, AND SHERLOCK HOLMES' LEGACY

During a week of mystery at Montreat Conference Center, uncover the secrets of the lives and works of Agatha Christie, Sir Arthur Conan Doyle, Alfred Hitchcock, and others.

ALASKA

Alaska is unmistakable proof that you don't have to leave the country to cross items off your travel bucket list. The state's supercharged land- and seascapes include massive glaciers, whales, and grizzlies. And you don't have to be a top-tier wilderness explorer in top physical condition to see some of the best sights. Alaskan cruises, which offer accessible accommodations for almost everyone, highlight coastal wonders and port cities such as Sitka and Juneau. "Flightseeing" and helicopter shore excursions offer breathtaking views of mountains, forests, and untamed rivers. A leisurely inland alternative to cruising is a ride on the Aurora Winter Train, which runs between Anchorage and Fairbanks from fall to spring—which also happens to be prime time for seeing the Northern Lights.

NEW ZEALAND AND AUSTRALIA

A million kilometers away. The landscapes of the South Pacific are diverse, ranging from the Great Barrier Reef and the rugged Outback of Australia to the sheep-dotted plains and cliff-lined fjords of New Zealand. You'll find sophisticated, multicultural cities as well as an irresistible, live-for-the-moment attitude.

INDONESIA, BALI

With picture-perfect beaches, lush greenery, waterfalls, countless magnificent temples, and much more, Bali is a paradise for all who visit. It's also inexpensive, so you'll have money left over for relaxing spa treatments like a Balinese massage with traditional herbs and spices. Ubud is a must-see destination, with markets and galleries, as well as the Ubud Palace and Sacred Monkey Forest. If you want to explore the entire island, you can hire a private driver to take you around while learning about the culture.

BARCELONA, THE FRENCH RIVIERA, AND THE ITALIAN RIVIERA

This trip includes memorable culture, architecture, and Mediterranean food, as well as sunny siestas in Barcelona and relaxing riposo in Italy. Sip sangria in front of La Sagrada Familia, stroll through medieval Avignon and visit seaside villages.

VOLUNTEER TO BE A CAMPGROUND HOST.

Many campgrounds and RV parks offer free campsites and amenities in exchange for assistance with tasks such as collecting fees, enforcing rules, and cleaning up after themselves. Campground hosting positions can last a few weeks or an entire season; they are typically volunteer positions, but some do pay a small stipend. This can be an excellent way to travel for less money.

BIKING TOUR OF GEORGIA'S ST. SIMONS AND JEKYLL IS-LANDS

Bike Explore St. Simons and Jekyll Islands with experts, visit a historic lighthouse, learn about coastal ecosystems, and enjoy authentic Southern culture and cuisine.

CAPE MAY, NEW JERSEY BIRDING

Cape May is a haven for both birds and birdwatchers., thanks to its many protected areas and diverse habitats. Visit in the spring to see songbirds and in the fall to see raptors!

SOUTH CAROLINA LOWCOUNTRY BIRDING

The Lowcountry of South Carolina is a haven for both birds and birders with its salt marshes, lush forests, coastal estuaries, and a variety of wildlife refuges

BIRDING THE EASTERN SHORE OF VIRGINIA AND CHIN-COTEAGUE ISLAND, VIRGINIA

Enjoy exclusive access to Wallops Island and other protected birding destinations, where you'll learn from experts while searching for the region's 400+ bird species.

BIRDS AND BLOOMS: SPRING IN MINNESOTA'S MISSISSIPPI RIVER VALLEY

Minnesota's Mississippi River Valley is the largest of North America's major flyways. Naturalists will take you to see warbler migrations, beautiful spring wildflowers, and Bald Eagles!

MISSOURI'S BRANSON

Branson has become one of the most popular senior vacation destinations, as well as a favorite among single senior travel groups, especially if you're active and enjoy outdoor activities. Among the activities available are golf, museums, shopping, live shows, and music. Among the activities available are golf, museums, shopping, live shows, and music. Branson, recently named "Live Music Show Capital of the World," is the best Las Vegas alternative. It is also much quieter, less expensive, and easier to navigate.

HIDDEN VALLEY BRIDGE IN CALIFORNIA

At Hidden Valley Institute, you will learn to properly evaluate your hand, master bidding conventions, and learn new techniques from experts as you immerse yourself in bridge.

THE PACIFIC COAST HIGHWAY IN CALIFORNIA

A road trip can be a fantastic way to spend your vacation, especially if you visit a new location. If you've never driven Highway One along the California coast, you should because it's one of the most beautiful drives in the world. The "Big Sur Coast," the stretch of highway between San Simeon and Carmel, is especially beautiful, with a number of inns and resorts where you can soak up ocean views from the comfort of your room. If the drive is too long, consider continuing north to San Francisco, Mendocino, or even further.

THE ROCKIES OF CANADA

The Canadian Rockies are another stunning natural landscape that can be easily appreciated from the comfort of a train car. The Rocky Mountaineer, which offers luxury rail journeys with gourmet meals, plush berths, and glass-domed carriages for unobstructed views of western Canada's imposing peaks and glacier-fed lakes so perfectly turquoise you'd swear they'd been Photoshopped, is the ultimate option. From Alberta to British Columbia, routes connect national parks, wildlife preserves, ski runs, and hiking trails in Jasper, Kamloops, and other mountain wonders.

BIRDING IN CAVE CREEK CANYON, ARIZONA'S PORTAL

Cave Creek Ranch is located in the Chiricahua Mountains of Southeastern Arizona, on 7 secluded acres alongside famous Cave Creek, and offers spectacular views of the rhyolite cliffs of Cave Creek Canyon.

RIVER CRUISES IN CENTRAL EUROPE

A river cruise is an excellent way for seniors to travel through scenic stretches of Germany, Austria, and Hungary via iconic European waterways such as the Danube and the Rhine. The pace on deck is leisurely, with scenic landscapes scrolling by like the world's most impressive stage backdrop. Of course, those looking for more action can opt for wine tastings, opera performances, and bike tours, many of which include electric-assist bikes for those who need a little extra pedal power on hills and steep medieval streets.

CENTRE FOR ITALIAN STUDIES IN TAORMINA

Study Italian language and culture at the Babilonia Italian Language School! Established in 1992, Babilonia is located in Taormina, a popular destination for many 19th and 20th-century creatives (Oscar Wilde, D.H. Lawrence, and Truman Capote, to name a few). Live with a local host family and test your language skills while taking a cooking class! Sicily tends to get skipped over in favor of mainland Italy, but this island is a powerhouse of culture, history, and delicious food (cannoli and arancini). Taormina itself is home to the ruins of a massive ancient Greek theatre and sits atop a mountain overlooking the Mediterranean Sea and Mt. Etna, one of Europe's highest active volcanoes. You'll be treated to stunning views while expanding your language skills!

SOUTH CAROLINA'S CHARLESTON

Charleston, dubbed the best city in the region, oozes history and hospitality, from charming buildings and walkways to friendly locals.Even those with limited mobility will be able to get around and connect with others thanks to the Southern city's diverse group tours, which range from ghostly graveyard walks to food tours to history lessons via horse-drawn carriage, boat, or bus. For a city so deeply linked to both the American Revolution and the Civil War, it's also surprisingly modern — its restaurant and boutique hotel scene is constantly reinventing itself, making it a popular weekend destination.

ILLINOIS, CHICAGO

After a hectic senior year, a trip to Chicago may be just what the doctor ordered. Visit famous landmarks such as Navy Pier and the Bean in Millennium Park, as well as world-class museums such as the Field Museum, Art Institute, and Adler Planetarium. Shop on the Magnificent Mile and meet some friendly sea creatures at the Shedd Aquarium.

CHINCOTEAGUE, VIRGINIA: LIGHTHOUSES, WILD PONIES, AND PIRATES

Virginia's only inhabited barrier island, as well as the national wildlife refuge and seashore, has breathtaking views, wild ponies, wildlife, miles of trails and beaches, and fascinating history.

COLUMBIA RIVER EXPLORER: A RELAXED RIVERBOAT ADVENTURE IN OREGON AND WASHINGTON

Travel along the Columbia River to learn about its fascinating history and breathtaking natural beauty. Trace Lewis and Clark's route, visit Portland landmarks, and sample local wines.

SLOW TRAVEL IN COSTA RICA: WATER AND LAND NATURAL WONDERS

Enjoy Costa Rica's natural history, biodiversity, and friendly attitude in a leisurely manner. This enables you to understand the true meaning of "Pura Vida."

RAINFORESTS, VOLCANOES, AND WILDLIFE IN COSTA RICA

Costa Rica is a true paradise. This Central American hotspot has it all, from misty cloud forests and lush jungles to volcanic landscapes and sun-kissed beaches. Begin your small group Adventure Tour in Tortuguero, known for its picturesque rainforest canals, before swimming in the natural hot springs at the foot of the mighty Arenal Volcano and exploring the majestic cloud forest region before concluding in San José.

NEVADA CRIME SCENE FORENSICS

On this true-crime adventure, you will discover the art of modern forensic science and meet with CSI professionals as you learn about fingerprinting and blood pattern analysis.

CLOSE THE CURTAINS! BROADWAY MUSICALS IN NORTH CAROLINA'S 'LAND OF THE SKY'

Discover your passion for Broadway music in the Blue Ridge Mountains. Get a behind-the-scenes look at musical theater and its glorious history with a show tunes expert at the piano.

FLORIDA'S DAYTONA BEACH

Begin your Daytona Beach vacation at the beach. When you've had your fill of relaxation, stop by the Jackie Robinson Ballpark for a quick game. Visit the Ponce de Leon Lighthouse for a chance at eternal youth, and then have some fun at the Boardwalk Amusement Area. Do you want some more action? Pass by the famous Daytona International Speedway before cooling off at Daytona Lagoon.

EXPLORE LONDON, PARIS, AND ROME.

Explore the history and culture of three inspiring and influential cities. Perhaps no cities have had a greater impact on the world in the last 2,000 years than Paris, London , and Rome. Eiffel Tower, the Big Ben, and the Colosseum are just a few of the iconic sights you'll see. Take it all in as you set out on this grand tour of France, England , and Italy.

PORTUGAL'S DOURO RIVER

The Douro Valley, a UNESCO World Heritage site and one of the world's oldest wine regions, has enchanting valleys and steep slopes that make it a premier wine destination. The Douro Valley, just a short drive from Porto and its famous Port wine aged in cellars across the river in Vila Nova de Gaia, is home to grapes that produce sweet red wines. Travel by train from Porto to Pocinho.

EGYPT AND THE NILE RIVER CRUISE

Sultans and souks, pharaohs and pyramids, temples and tombs Descend into a world of ancient wonders to learn about the lands that inspired legends. Walk through sphinx avenues and royal valleys amid the desert sands, past towering stone icons. Then, cruise down the Nile, stopping at remote islands and next to the Theban Hills. End your journey in Cairo, where historic mosques coexist with modern bustle.

ROAD TRIP FOR FOOD

Vacations are all about indulging, and one of the best ways to do so is to try new cuisine. A food road trip makes travel more appealing by providing the opportunity to sample local delicacies. Road trips are also one of the most accessible modes of transportation for people with limited mobility, and with some planning and preparation, accessible road trips can be truly amazing! If you've never considered including some food destinations in your travel itinerary, now is the time. Consider what foods you would be willing to travel for. What about a pizza tour in Chicago or a barbecue road trip? You should plan your trip around your absolute favorite food. If you're a fan of Philly cheese steak, why not go to its birthplace? You'll be able to sample the best of what you enjoy.

Visit the most famous food destinations to find out what all the fuss is about. If you're not sure where to begin, look at what other foodies think are the best. If you enjoy food but are unsure what to eat, check Yelp reviews or other review sites such as TripAdvisor for the best restaurants.

Customize your own food tour—whether it's a self-curated Wisconsin cheese tour or a few New Hampshire ice cream stops—you're sure to be satisfied with a trip you've designed.

CHAUTAUQUA'S FOREIGN POLICY NEW YORK-BASED AMERICAN FOREIGN SERVICE

Explore the complex issues of US diplomacy alongside ambassadors and foreign service officers while listening to lectures and gaining insider knowledge.

FLORENCE GELATO COURSE

This creamy delectableness outperforms ice cream. Gelato is a work of art in and of itself, and you can now learn how to make authentic Italian gelato in Florence, a city known for producing masterpieces. The Florence Culinary Arts School not only teaches you how to make gelato but also how to run your own gelateria (what a great retirement plan!). Housing is provided, as are optional Italian lessons. And, of course, there are numerous opportunities for taste testing!

AUSTRIA, GERMANY, AND SWITZERLAND

Germany, Switzerland, and Austria all speak the same language, but their appeals differ. Discover each destination's delightfully distinct style and substance, from the Gothic spires of Heidelberg to the Art Nouveau elegance of Vienna. The Swiss Alps and the Bavarian Forest, German beer and Austrian wine—this trio of countries offers something for everyone on tour.

ENGLAND, SCOTLAND, AND IRELAND HIGHLIGHTS

Explore the emerald landscapes and cultural centers of the United Kingdom and Ireland. Travel from cosmopolitan London to the medieval city of Edinburgh on a guided tour of England, Scotland, and Ireland. Then, as you travel between Scotland and Ireland, stop in the Lake District and Wales. When you arrive in Ireland, grab a pint (or a few) with Dubliners and make your way along the scenic Ring of Kerry and Cliffs of Moher, taking in the stunning sea views along the way.

HORSEMANSHIP BASICS AND BEYOND IN MISSOURI'S OZARKS

Prepare to saddle up and ride! Enjoy the peaceful forests of the Ozark Mountains while learning about equine behavior, grooming, saddling, and horseback riding.

GEORGIA'S JEKYLL ISLAND

You might not have heard of Jekyll Island, but it could be the perfect retirement location for you. For baby boomers and retirees, Jekyll Island offers a variety of appealing activities. There are beaches, fishing, biking, tennis, golf, and even Sunday dinner dances. The Grand Dining Room at the Jekyll Island Club Hotel, for example, hosts events where guests can dine on gourmet cuisine and dance the night away - a romantic option for retired couples.

HAWAII'S KAUAI

Kauai has something for everyone, regardless of age. There's plenty to do for those who prefer to take in the breathtaking scenery rather than surf the powerful waves, including visits to botanical gardens. This is, after all, the "Garden Isle." A favorite is Limanhuli Gardens & Preserve. It has been named the country's No. 1 natural botanical garden, with riparian habitat and pristine forest, including rare native ferns, palms, and culturally significant plants like taro and papaya. There are lighthouses to see and beautiful beaches to relax on. Don't miss the Waimea Canyon Lookout, and if you're visiting during the winter, consider taking a whale-watching tour.

FLORIDA'S KEY WEST

The Florida Keys, which stretch over 125 miles from Biscayne National Park in the north to Key West, provide some of the best opportunities for sailing and other water sports of any destination in America. Key West is the jewel of the crown. It's also one of the best places to visit if you prefer a slower pace of life, so whatever type of vacation you're looking for, you'll find it here. Sunsets are spectacular, and one of the best ways to see them is on a sunset sailing cruise, but if you prefer to stay on land, watching the sunset from the dock at Mallory Square is also unforgettable. You'll also be able to take a day trip to Dry Tortugas National Park, which is famous for its world-class snorkeling, and sample delectable Cuban-inspired cuisine at any of the hundreds of restaurants that line the island's main beachfront.

IMMERSION IN KHMER CULTURE IN CAMBODIA

Participate in community development projects in Cambodia to go beyond the typical tourist experience! Projects Abroad is dedicated to providing safe, stress-free, and life-changing travel experiences. There are numerous trips available for active seniors to choose from. You could, for example, assist in the provision of medical services in a rural village or teach English in kindergartens in under-resourced schools. Volunteering in Cambodia is an excellent way to become acquainted with the Khmer culture.

Projects Abroad can even assist you in learning some of the local languages! Other cultural activities include making puppets and pottery, Apsara dance classes, and tasting some delicious Cambodian chicken curry.

BIRDING THE ISLANDS AND SHORES OF LAKE ERIE, OHIO

When it comes to bird migrations, there is no place like the Lake Erie Islands: beautiful trees, blue skies, and a plethora of birds passing through. Bring your binoculars; this one's a keeper!

CALIFORNIA, LOS ANGELES

See what movie magic inspires at Universal Studios Park, locate your favorite celebrity's star on the Hollywood Walk of Fame, and visit the Kodak Theater, where the Oscars are held each year. Take a break from the glitz and spend some time at the beach, or visit Chinatown, Disneyland, and Six Flags Magic Mountain. In Los Angeles, there is something for every celebrity.

PERU'S MACHU PICCHU

Hiking along the Inca Trail is an epic way to approach Peru's mysterious citadel in the Andes. However, if an arduous trek at high altitudes does not appeal to you, you do not have to cross Machu Picchu off your bucket list. A train from Cusco will also take you there, with spectacular views of lush valleys and snow-capped peaks along the way. A guided group tour can help with not only planning and meeting specific needs but also meeting new people.

FLORIDA'S MIAMI

Consider visiting Miami Beach if you're looking for warmth, sunshine, beautiful stretches of sand, and plenty of culture. It has a lot to offer retirees and travelers of all kinds. There are numerous fantastic museums, such as the Wolfsonian-FIU Museum, and an abundance of shopping opportunities in the city itself, in addition to endless picturesque beaches and outstanding beachfront resorts. Fairchild Tropical Botanic Garden, regarded as one of the best in the country, is only a few minutes away.

CALIFORNIA'S MONTEREY JAZZ FESTIVAL

Join the cool cats at the Monterey Jazz Festival for world-class performances, informative lectures, and panel discussions in the historical setting of Monterey.

CALIFORNIA'S MORRO BAY

Morro Bay is a lovely beach town on the central California coast with interesting shops to explore, restaurants serving fresh seafood, uncrowded stretches of sand, and vineyards to visit. It's famous for its abundant marine life, which includes whales that can be seen year-round and an active sea otter population that lives in the water just offshore. Kayaking, beachcombing, picnicking, birdwatching, and hiking are also available.

CALIFORNIA NATIONAL ROAD SCHOLAR RECORDER/ EARLY MUSIC WORKSHOP

Improve your recorder, viola da gamba, or reeds skills in large and small ensembles with world-class instructors — and cap off your week with a concert in picturesque Carmel Valley!

VOLUNTEERING IN ARIZONA, NAVAJO NATION SCHOOLS

"We do not inherit the land from our ancestors; we borrow it from our children," says a Navajo proverb. Volunteer in schools on the Navajo Reservation to give back.

LOUISIANA'S NEW ORLEANS AT A SLOWER PACE: A CITY OF HISTORY, CULTURE, AND CELEBRATION

Explore New Orleans' historic districts, learn about Cajun cooking, and visit the famed National World War II Museum to learn about art and heritage.

THE CITY OF NEW YORK

Of course, the magnificent Big Apple is our most popular senior trip destination. Central Park, Rockefeller Plaza, Times Square, the Statue of Liberty, Broadway, the 9/11 Memorial, and Chinatown are among the most popular attractions.

NEWFOUNDLAND

The easternmost province of Canada has a lot to see and do, as well as some of the friendliest people on the planet. St. John's, its historic capital city, is the oldest in North America, with colorful homes and buildings housing galleries, museums, specialty shops, and pubs hosting live music every night of the week. Trinity, a few hours away, maybe the most beautiful town you've ever seen, looking as if it was built for a movie set. Icebergs frequently float by or land in one of the many picturesque coves in the mid-to-late spring, while humpback whales can be seen in large numbers during the summer. Elliston, a short drive north, is one of the best places in the world to see puffins up close, sometimes within arms' reach.

THE NIAGARA FALLS

The beauty of Niagara Falls cannot be overstated. This magnificent wonder is located on the border between Canada and the United States. If you are not driving, the best option is to fly to Buffalo Niagara International Airport. Amtrak also provides service to the falls. Take the famous Maid of the Mist Boat Tour from the New York side of the falls for the best views and experience. If you're feeling daring, consider taking the Cave of The Winds Tour (an elevator ride down 175 feet into the Niagara Gorge). A bus tour is also available.

MARYLAND'S OCEAN CITY

Enjoy free beach access to rest and relax, then spend some time strolling the famous Boardwalk. Take an Assateague Eco-Cruise, ride the rides at Jolly Roger Amusement Park, and work your way through a massive maze at Planet Maze Lastertron for a day of adventure. Don't forget to visit the Ocean City Life Saving Station, which is part of the Coastal System established by the United States Treasury Department to save vessels in distress and lives in peril on the waters, and round out your trip with a visit to the strange and strange. Believe It Or Not! Ripley's Believe It Or Not!

OREGON AMERICAN MUSIC FESTIVAL, OREGON

Attend concerts, films, lectures, and access rehearsals at the Oregon Festival of American Music if you love music!

PAR FOR THE COURSE: GOLFING ON JEKYLL ISLAND, GEORGIA

With Georgia's largest public golf resort, experienced golf professionals, and three renowned 18-hole golf courses, Jekyll Island is the place to improve your golf game.

CZECH REPUBLIC, PRAGUE

Prague is well-known for its diverse architecture and museums, as well as its plentiful and inexpensive nightlife and extensive shopping options. It is also known for its hearty food and cheap beer, as well as its well-kept

UNESCO World Heritage city center.

MONTREAL, QUEBEC, CANADA

When you step onto Quebec City's cobblestone streets, you might think you've landed in Europe. It exudes Old World charm throughout its top attractions, thanks to its French culture and 17th-century ramparts. While French is spoken here, most locals also speak English, so getting around or ordering a cafe au lait and a crepe is simple. You can watch Canadian troops perform a military ceremony at the citadel before sipping afternoon tea at the Chateau Frontenac. The magnificent Notre Dame Basilica is a must-see, and there are numerous parks to stroll through. A stunning 272-foot-high waterfall can be found just a few miles north in Montmorency Falls Park.

RANCHO DE LA OSA: RANCH LIFE ON ARIZONA'S SOUTHERN BORDER

Experience life at Arizona's most historic ranch. Enjoy peaceful trail rides near the Buenos Aires Wildlife Refuge while learning about horse grooming, ranch crafts, and ancient history.

RENT OR PURCHASE A TRAILER OR MOTOR-HOME AND HIT THE ROAD.

Set a goal of dipping your toes in each ocean, driving the length of Route 66, or visiting every national park in the country. If you're over the age of 62, you can get a lifetime federal park pass for only $80; in some cases, the pass also includes substantial discounts on camping and boat launch fees.

TEXAS, SAN ANTONIO

Texas cities are extremely affordable for those traveling within the United

States. San Antonio, in particular, is a must-see destination in the state, having been ranked No. 9 in Best Affordable Destinations in the USA by US News & World Report and recently named the most affordable "foodie city" by WalletHub. San Antonio is a unique place to visit because of the Alamo historic site (the five area missions are Texas' only UNESCO World Heritage site) and the nearby Natural Bridge Caverns. San Antonio, with its famous River Walk, is also ideal for pedestrians.

SAN DIEGO, CALIFORNIA, FROM AQUARIUM TO ZOO

You and your grandchildren can learn about animals by going underwater and behind the scenes at the San Diego Zoo and Birch Aquarium. At the beach, you can also ride a boogie board and a roller coaster.

MEXICO, SAN MIGUEL DE ALLENDE

San Miguel de Allende, twice named the "best city in the world" by Travel + Leisure magazine, has colonial charm, a thriving culinary scene with organic farm-to-table eateries, art galleries, shops selling handcrafted items, and relaxing hot springs. It's so appealing (and safe) that many retirees and others from around the world have chosen to live there. The historic center, a UNESCO World Heritage Site, is filled with well-preserved buildings from the 17th and 18th centuries, and it's fun just to wander through the narrow cobbled streets and leafy courtyards.

NEW MEXICO'S SANTA FE

Santa Fe's Spanish Colonial adobe buildings and magical setting in the foothills of the rose-tinted Sangre de Cristo Mountains have drawn artists and other scenery seekers for generations. A warm, dry climate and a compact and walkable historic downtown centered on a leafy plaza dating back to the early 1600s are additional draws for the 65-and-up crowd.

There are numerous art galleries, museums honoring the region's rich Native American traditions, and restaurants serving Southwestern cuisine within walking distance. Depending on the time of year, rugged types can go skiing or hiking in the surrounding mountains.

SCANDINAVIAN CAPITALS AND FJORDS

Discover the wonders of Northern Europe. Scandinavia has a lot to offer, from seafaring histories to breathtaking fjords. Admire Norway's stunning green cliffs and blue water before setting sail from Oslo to Denmark's waterside capital. Explore the remaining Nordic capitals, including Stockholm and Helsinki, two of the world's most livable cities, and learn about their maritime histories and modern architecture.

ARIZONA'S SEDONA

Sedona is a short two-hour drive from Phoenix and is easily accessible from many cities in the United States. Located in a geological wonderland, with multi-colored red rock formations that change color minute by minute as the light and weather change. The scenery is breathtaking, and the mild climate makes outdoor activities even more enjoyable. Jeep tours, hiking, and bird watching are just a few of the activities available. There are world-class spas, stunning resorts, a vibrant art scene, and a New Age vibe in town, with all kinds of shops and services offering alternative cures for whatever ails you.

YOGA, QI GONG, AYURVEDA, AND OTHER HEALING ARTS FOR WOMEN IN SEDONA, ARIZONA

Join other women in Sedona's inspiring setting to learn about and practice a variety of healing techniques that focus on mind, body, spiritual well-being, and longevity.

ITALY'S SICILY

Sicily is an Italian island in the Mediterranean Sea with breathtaking sea views. It's also one of the Italian destinations recommended for retirees by Leo Locke, president of Italian travel tour operator Donna Franca Tours, along with Malta and the Amalfi Coast. By taking a Sicilian tour, you can see the Valley of the Temples, go wine tasting, and eat delicious Italian fare like arancini (Sicilian rice balls), caponata (an eggplant stew), and, of course, pizza.

SOUTH AFRICAN REPUBLIC

Who wouldn't want to see lions, elephants, giraffes, and zebras in their natural habitat? The good news is that wildlife-viewing tours are conducted in all-terrain vehicles rather than on foot, which is ideal for older travelers with limited physical abilities. The ride can be bumpy, so for the sake of your joints, choose a game preserve with a well-oiled tourism infrastructure that can accommodate a diverse range of visitors. As a result, the Kruger National Park in South Africa is an obvious choice. After you've seen the Big 5 (lions, leopards, rhinos, elephants, and Cape buffaloes), you can take advantage of the dollar-friendly exchange rate to explore other parts of South Africa. Choose from vineyard tours, beach vacations, and the tram ride up Table Mountain in Cape Town. Your once-in-a-lifetime vacation could be the first of many.

AFRICA'S SOUTHERNMOST CONTINENT SOUTH AFRICA, ZAMBIA, ZIMBABWE, AND BOTSWANA BIRDING SAFARI

Add Southern African birds to your life list as you explore four countries' diverse habitats with experts, observing rare wildlife and learning about local culture.

WASHINGTON, DC: SPIES, LIES, AND INTELLIGENCE: THE WORLD OF INTERNATIONAL ESPIONAGE.

With intelligence experts, tour the nation's capital and its museums to learn about espionage history and 21st-century intelligence threats.

FLORIDA'S ST. AUGUSTINE

For history buffs, America's oldest continuously occupied European settlement is a must-see, where they can explore what remains of more than two centuries of Spanish rule, beginning in 1565. For those who can't walk far, a compact, magnolia-lined historic district makes it easy to see the sights. It's even easier with convenient hop-on, hop-off sightseeing trolleys (often with buy-one, get-one discounts for those over 55).

GO ON A CRUISE.

Do you want to spend your vacation on the water? Cruises are popular among retirees because they provide a nearly all-inclusive experience that allows you to visit new places every day. And, contrary to popular belief, cruising may be less expensive than you think: major lines such as Carnival and Royal Caribbean offer discounts on certain sailings for travelers over the age of 55.

GOLF ON THE GULF COAST: LEARN FROM THE ORIGINAL GOLF SCHOOL IN FLORIDA'S PROS

Custom-tailored golf lessons and daily instruction from the Original Golf School will help you improve your swing, situational play, and on-course etiquette.

THAILAND

Thailand is an enticing choice for seniors seeking variety, culture, and a little relaxation, with its beaches, Buddhist temples, floating markets, and the nonstop excitement of Bangkok. The locals' reverence for elders is an added bonus.

THAILAND BABY ELEPHANT ADVENTURE

Travel to the Land of Smiles with Discover Corps and assist in the care of baby elephants at an elephant nursery! You'll work alongside mahouts, the traditional expert elephant caregivers, and help with everything from feeding to bathing. Thailand is a must-see for any world traveler, regardless of age. This itinerary includes excursions to Chiang Mai's ancient temples and bustling markets, Northern Thailand's beautiful countryside and vibrant jungles, and the famous Thai food markets. You'll be unable to keep that grin off your face!

NORTH CAROLINA, THE BEAUTIFUL AND POWERFUL OF THE ITALIAN RENAISSANCE

The Medici, the Mona Lisa, and St. Peter's Basilica are all iconic Italian structures, but how did they come to be? Investigate and debate the Italian Renaissance's origins, artists, and legacy.

SOUTH CAROLINA'S BEST BARBECUE: SECRET RECIPES, SAUCES, AND SMOKERS

BBQ is more than just a way of life for some people. Visit an experienced Pit-Master for an in-depth look at their culinary craft and see for yourself.

GLACIER NATIONAL PARK, MONTANA'S BEST

Explore Glacier National Park by rafting the Flathead River, hiking alpine trails, visiting pristine lakes, and learning about how glaciers carved this stunning landscape eons ago.

THE MISSISSIPPI RIVER'S BEST: A JOURNEY INTO SOUTHERN HERITAGE, LOUISIANA/MISSISSIPPI/TENNESSEE

Explore the Mississippi River on a paddlewheel riverboat while listening to jazz, learning about Civil War history, and having fun in New Orleans!

THE CARIBBEAN ISLANDS

With its velvety sands, sky-blue waters, and flip-flop-friendly weather, the Caribbean is an ideal destination for unwinding. Those who have difficulty getting around may want to take an ocean cruise to see the region. All of the major cruise lines have worked to improve the accessibility of their ships and excursions for all passengers.

NEW YORK'S CHAUTAUQUA EXPERIENCE IN THE FALL AND SPRING

The Chautauqua Institution, founded in 1874, is a long-lasting celebration of art, history, and culture. Classes, lectures, and expert-led excursions await you here for an enriching adventure.

CHINCOTEAGUE, ASSATEAGUE, AND WALLOPS ISLANDS ON VIRGINIA'S EASTERN SHORE

Explore the wonders of Virginia's Eastern Shore islands while visiting local museums, seeing the wild ponies of Assateague, and having exclusive access to unspoiled Wallops Island.

THE SCOTS-IRISH LEGACY: FROM HISTORICAL MIGRATION TO CULTURAL INSPIRATION, NORTH CAROLINA

Explore the Scots-Irish contributions to Appalachian culture, Civil War history, and the drafting of the Declaration of Independence to learn how they helped shape our nation.

C. S. LEWIS'S LIFE AND WORKS: INSPIRATION, BELIEF, AND THE POWER OF LANGUAGE, NORTH CAROLINA

View the world through C. S. Lewis's eyes as you join experts to view and discuss rare materials, listen to a broadcast from his Oxford days, and take a virtual tour of his England home.

AMELIA ISLAND, BAHAMAS, CHARLESTON, AND MORE IN FLORIDA BY SMALL SHIP

Travel along the Atlantic Ocean on a fascinating small-ship learning adventure that takes you from Florida to Georgia, South Carolina, and the Bahamas.

HOUSES OF COMMERCE.

Exchange houses with other travelers to get completely free vacation accommodations. House swapping allows you to live like a local and provides an immersive experience. Whether you want a weekend getaway in a nearby region or an extended vacation abroad, there are options for you. Websites for older adults include Home Exchange 50plus and HomeExchange.com.

TULUM (MEXICO)

Tulum is a peaceful, secluded beach town with clear, blue water and plenty of activities for retirees.

If you enjoy an active lifestyle as a retiree, Tulum has it all: biking, beach walking, yoga, swimming, diving, or simply relaxing in a spa.

ITALY'S TUSCANY

Many people want to visit Tuscany, and retirees will find plenty to do here. Stay in the heart of Florence, the "Cradle of the Renaissance," or opt for a more affordable stay in the countryside, surrounded by vineyards and olive groves. Wine tours of all kinds are available, including private and small group tours that can take you to the best wineries and allow you to meet some of the winemakers and sample local delicacies. Relax in picturesque squares, gaze up at centuries-old palazzos and cathedrals, or simply soak up the Tuscan sun amidst breathtaking scenery.

PARKS IN THE UNITED STATES

What about a ranger-led nature walk among Yellowstone's geysers? Or how about a scenic drive through the Great Smoky Mountains, past forests, wildflowers, and possibly a black bear or two? The wonders of the United States national park system are accessible to visitors of all inclinations and physical abilities, from those who peer into the Grand Canyon from the rim to those who paddle through it on a canoe.

ARIZONA'S ULTIMATE OLD WEST EXPERIENCE: THE WHITE STALLION RANCH

Discover your pioneer spirit while enjoying scenic trail rides, ranching demonstrations, country western dance lessons, and cowboy songs around an evening bonfire on a working dude ranch.

VIETNAM/CAMBODIA

Many retirees want to visit places that were once considered unattainable in the not-too-distant past. These places include Cambodia and Vietnam, which he recommends retirees visit by taking a Mekong River cruise. Excursions in Vietnam and Cambodia can include visiting the Cu Chi Tunnels of Viet Cong fighters in Ho Chi Minh City or Angkor Wat in Cambodia.

BEACH, VIRGINIA

After a relaxing day in the sand, visit the infamous Boardwalk and do some shopping on Atlantic Avenue. Take an American Rover Student Party Cruise for a fantastic party complete with professional DJs and delectable dining. Make a splash at Ocean Breeze Water Park or take a short trip to Busch Gardens in nearby Williamsburg.

VISIT ALL 50 STATES OF THE UNITED STATES

If you like to "conquer the vacation," visiting all 50 states is the ultimate vacation bucket list. Whether you want to explore the country's natural beauty or indulge in unique regional cuisine, the United States has it all.

2 WEEKS OF VOLUNTEER WORK IN PERU

Many travel programs are now combining volunteer work with traditional tourism, and Máximo Nivel has discovered a pretty good formula for success: spend one-week volunteering and one week traveling and exploring Peru! Volunteer opportunities range from animal care to working with marginalized indigenous communities. You will also receive two hours of Spanish classes while volunteering. This all-inclusive package includes visits to Cusco, Machu Picchu, the Sacred Valley of the Incas, and Lake Titicaca!

IN GERMANY, YOU CAN HELP REFUGEES BY VOLUNTEERING.

Spend some time at the Halle Excellence Center, Germany, to put your travel experience to good use. You'll be able to immerse yourself in the rich history of Halle, the birthplace of famous Baroque composer George Frideric Handel, while also engaging meaningfully with the local community. Throughout this program, you will teach English to many refugees who arrive in Germany eager to improve their English skills. You'll also be able to improve your Arabic skills with free Arabic lessons!

THE NATION'S CAPITAL IS WASHINGTON, DC.

Every American should visit Washington, DC at least once in their lives because there are so many cultural, architectural, and historical landmarks to see. Many notable museums, such as the National Museum of Natural History and the National Air and Space Museum, are free to enter, and visiting iconic memorials along the National Mall, among other free activities, can provide budget-conscious travelers with a lot of bang for their buck. A hop-on, hop-off sightseeing tour — or even a night tour of the capital city's illuminated monuments and memorials — is a cheap, flexible, and relatively simple way to navigate the city's plethora of attractions.

TONI CHAPLIN'S WATERCOLOR WORKSHOP IN THE PO-CONOS, PENNSYLVANIA

Toni Chaplin's unique teaching style and insightful approach will inspire your creativity and help you improve your watercolor skills alongside the beautiful Delaware River.

WILDLIFE, WALKING, AND HIKING IN VERMONT'S GREEN MOUNTAIN STATE

Explore Vermont's picturesque woodlands on expert-led walks and hikes, and learn about the fascinating local wildlife and history.

VIRGINIA'S WILLIAMSBURG

If you enjoy history, you'll enjoy Williamsburg. You'll be able to experience what it was like to be an original settler by staying in one of the 26 Colonial Houses scattered throughout the historic area, which range from a tavern room to a two-bedroom. Take a walking tour to see the saddle maker, blacksmith, wigmaker, and apothecary, and meet historical figures like one of the Founding Fathers or First Lady Martha Washington along the way. Costumed characters portray the details of life in early America, providing a glimpse into a time period that a history book could never provide. There are also many great shops, museums, and other fun things to do in the area, many of which offer senior discounts.

BUENOS AIRES WINE PROGRAM

Spend some time sipping in Buenos Aires at one of Argentina's most renowned wine programs. You'll learn wine tasting techniques, pairings, varieties, and flavors with Mente Argentina—everything you need to know to impress your friends when you return home! The Argentine Malbec is just one of 50 unique Argentine and international wines you'll discover. Courses range from a two-week intensive to a month-long wine-ding journey through Argentina's countryside. Mente Argentina caters to solo travelers in particular by organizing meet-ups with other participants, making this one of the best tours for seniors traveling alone. Meet your fellow wine enthusiasts on the dance floor or in a Spanish class!

OBSERVE THE NORTHERN LIGHTS

Seeing the kaleidoscopic Northern Lights, also known as the aurora borealis, is a once-in-a-lifetime opportunity for many travelers, given that appearances can be unpredictable due to weather, darkness, and solar activity. However, there are numerous exciting locations to view the spectacular natural light show. Guided tours are available from Alaska to Sweden for those interested in this remarkable natural phenomenon — as well as other energizing outdoor activities such as husky trekking in the Arctic wilderness and soaks in hot mineral springs.

DONATE YOUR TIME

"IT'S NOT HOW MUCH WE GIVE, BUT HOW MUCH LOVE
WE PUT INTO GIVING."

-MOTHER TERESA-

Volunteering provides you with a sense of purpose and allows you to contribute to the greater good. According to the Transamerica Center for Retirement Studies, nearly one-quarter of retirees volunteer on a regular basis. Determine the types of organizations that interest you and see if they can make use of your skills.

Look into VolunteerMatch to find opportunities in your area. (Alternatively, consider international opportunities: there is no age limit for joining the Peace Corps!)

You could try:

COLLABORATE WITH MEALS ON WHEELS

Even in times of economic prosperity, hunger and malnutrition affect families across the United States and around the world, and the need for hunger relief becomes even more pressing during times of recession and high unemployment. As the number of families requesting food assistance increases, seniors make up a growing proportion of both the population seeking assistance and the volunteers providing it. Northwest Harvest, a hunger relief organization that serves all of Washington state, serves nearly 20% of its clients over the age of 55, and people over the age of 65 make up the vast majority of its volunteer force.

Seniors have long provided assistance to other seniors through Meals on Wheels, a network of nutrition programs dedicated to preventing hunger and malnutrition in the senior population in all 50 states and territories. Every day, up to 1.7 million volunteers, many of whom are retirees, deliver more than one million meals to seniors in need.

TEACH ENGLISH TO IMMIGRANTS

VOLUNTEER TO BE A SCOUT LEADER.

BUILD A HOUSE WITH HABITAT FOR HUMANITY

Habitat for Humanity is a non-profit organization that constructs and re-pairs simple, affordable housing with (rather than for!) people in need. Habitat volunteers work alongside those who have qualified to purchase a Habitat for Humanity home, assisting in the construction of not only houses but also a sense of pride and community for the new homeowners and their neighbors.

Many retired and semi-retired volunteers help Habitat for Humanity on construction sites, in disaster relief areas, and in affiliate offices. The ma-jority of the 6,000 registered "*RV Care-A-Vanners*," who drive their own RVs to participate in Habitat for Humanity homebuilding projects across the United States are retirees. *RV Care-A-Vanners* pay for their own trans-portation, but travel expenses related to their service are often tax deduct-ible.

Other places that might benefit from your assistance include:

LIBRARIES:

- Sort books

- Plan special events and fundraisers

- Deliver library materials to home-bound adults

HOSPICES:

- Support patients by visiting with them

- Reading to them

- Taking walks with them.

SENIORS' CENTERS:

- Greet patrons at the front desk

- Help out in the kitchen.

- Teach a computer class

THEATERS:

Distribute playbills and direct people to their seats (and possibly see a show for free).

CHURCHES OR OTHER HOUSES OF WORSHIP:

- Organize and direct community outreach projects

- Organize youth programs

MUSEUMS:

- Lead tours

- Answer questions from the public about exhibits

SHELTERS FOR ANIMALS:

For those who are unable to commit to owning a pet, volunteering at an animal shelter can provide a furry fix.

Volunteers are always needed at local animal shelters, rescues, and humane societies to:

- Feed and groom animals

- Clean cages

- Walk dogs

- Organize fundraising events

- Perform administrative tasks

- Help to rescue pets in the wake of floods, fires, and other natural disasters.

Foster parent: Retirees with the time and space to care for an animal may consider serving as a "foster parent" until a permanent placement for a homeless dog or cat can be found.

Animal shelters, like many other non-profit organizations, need:

- Grant writers

- Legal advocates

- Graphic designers to assist them in spreading the word about animal protection issues

Pet therapy: Pet owners should think about getting their pets certified through a pet therapy training program, which allows them to visit patients in nursing homes, children's hospitals, and hospice care.

FOOD BANKS:

- Receive shipments

- Sort food items

- Prepare packages

- Collecting, serving, preparing, or distributing food

VETERANS HOMES:

- Help with craft activities

- Play music with residents

- Escort veterans to appointments

- Helping Troops and Military Families

There are numerous opportunities for retired military personnel and civilian retirees who want to help veterans or active servicemen and women.

The USO's mission is to improve the quality of life for military personnel and their families in the United States and abroad. USO volunteers assist with everything from greeting troops returning from overseas tours and making hot coffee in USO offices to providing warm meals and blankets to troops on airport layovers while they wait for flights home.

The Veterans Affairs Volunteer Service Program (VAVS) of the Military Order of the Purple Heart assists wounded veterans and also others throughout the VA medical care system. VAVS volunteers also assist homeless veterans and help to honor veterans by creating and maintaining shrines and tributes in collaboration with the National Cemetery Administration.

OTHER COMMON FORMS OF VOLUNTEERING ARE:

- Fundraising or selling items to raise money

- Engaging in general labor, like helping build homes or clean up parks

- Tutoring or teaching

- Mentoring the youth

- Collecting, making, or distributing clothing

WORKING WITH CHILDREN

Most volunteer opportunities involving children will necessitate a background check as well as a commitment to volunteer for a set number of hours per week for a set period of time, such as three, six, or twelve months.

Volunteering with children can be both financially and personally rewarding in some cases: some foster grandparent volunteers are eligible for a tax-free hourly stipend, and an increasing number of public school districts offer seniors a property tax rebate in exchange for their time volunteering in the classroom.

Senior Corps Foster Grandparent program

Volunteers in the Senior Corps Foster Grandparent program work with children in Head Start centers, schools, and other youth facilities.

Retirees who live far away from their grandchildren (or who are patiently waiting for their grown children to produce some) may benefit most from volunteering with children.

Big Brothers Big Sisters organization

The Big Brothers Big Sisters organization provides adult volunteers ("bigs") with the opportunity to form long-term one-on-one relationships with children who require the presence of caring adults in their lives.

Children's Hospital

Many children's hospitals rely on volunteers for tasks such as tutoring patients, reading stories, monitoring playrooms, and assisting families with whatever they may require while their child is in the hospital.

DISASTER RELIEF

- Red Cross

Volunteers from the American Red Cross fly across the country and around the world to help residents affected by various types of disasters.

Devastating natural disasters such as the 2010 earthquake in Haiti, the 2011 earthquake and tsunami in Japan, and the devastating 2011 tornadoes in Alabama and Georgia have highlighted the need for specially trained volunteers to respond to all types of natural disasters. While disaster relief volunteers are frequently required to maintain certifications such as CPR or other lifesaving skills. But volunteers are also needed to handle supplies, donations, and administrative tasks, as well as provide comfort and assistance to crisis survivors.

- Medical Reserve Corps

Retired physicians, EMTs, nurses, pharmacists, and other medical professionals can also volunteer for the Medical Reserve Corps, a volunteer disaster relief organization run by the Surgeon General of the United States. Volunteers, including retirees, are also needed by the Medical Reserve Corps to work as interpreters, chaplains, office workers, and legal advisers, among other things.

- Docent or Tour Guide

Seniors have many opportunities during their retirement years to turn life-long hobbies into full-time volunteer pursuits and also to learn more about topics that have long piqued their interest. Museums, universities, and other public and private organizations frequently offer docent programs, which train volunteers to lead tours, preserve landmarks, and educate visitors. Many historical sites, botanical gardens, and land conservation organizations provide similar learning opportunities for volunteers.

Even retirees with seemingly esoteric interests or skills may be surprised at the number of volunteer opportunities available in their preferred fields. Volunteers are required to:

- Drive and maintain antique steam cars

- Rehabilitate birds of prey

- Lead tours of Kentucky's largest equestrian-themed park

- Political Campaigns

Baby boomers have a long history of activism, having taken part in the Civil Rights Movement, marched in numerous Vietnam and Gulf War protests, advocated for the Equal Rights Amendment and contributed to thousands of lesser-known causes. Many retirees will feel right at home volunteering for a political campaign, grassroots organization, or political action committee in support of a candidate or cause they believe in.

- Legal Advocate

Legal representation is required by organizations of all types, whether to advocate on behalf of the populations they serve but also to represent the organizations themselves in contract negotiations and other civil or business matters. Legal volunteers may be asked to advocate for foster children, defend minorities' rights, or represent battered spouses in domestic violence cases. Volunteer attorneys also represent environmental organizations, public lands trusts, animal rights organizations, and even developing-nation governments working to advance human rights and economic development.

Retirees with legal backgrounds bring valuable skills and experience to their roles in administrative offices and on non-profit boards of directors.

WRITING FOR FUN

With more time for thinking and reflection, you may discover that you have unique stories or know-how to share with the world. Writing can help you document memories, relieve stress, and work through emotions. Writing is also an effective way for seniors to keep their minds active as they age. It's simple to do, stimulates the mind, and provides numerous avenues to explore, ranging from prose to poetry.

TAKE A TRIP DOWN MEMORY LANE

Writing down memories is a fun and stimulating hobby. It keeps special memories from fading by writing them down so they can revisit them later. Writing down memories also helps with recall. The brain has to actively work to remember the details, which improves overall cerebral performance.

EMBRACE THE JOYS OF POETRY

Poetry is yet another effective and enjoyable way to use writing. Poetry's power lies in its simplicity. Poetry is about beauty. As a result, rather than requiring extensive planning, writing poetry allows seniors to express themselves freely. Because there is no beginning, middle, or end but just sentences that sound lovely.

CRAFT A STORY FROM START TO FINISH

Storytelling is one of the best ways to keep the mind stimulated through writing. According to Martin Lotze of the University of Greifswald in Germany, the creative process of crafting a story stimulates different parts of the brain than simply copying out text. As a result, creating an entirely new narrative necessitates thought and creativity, which increases mental agility.

WRITE A GOOD OLD-FASHIONED LETTER

While many people believe that letter writing is dead, it is still a valuable exercise that keeps the mind sharp. It's straightforward and sincere, so it's worth exploring.

WRITE YOUR DAILY ROUTINE

What was the happiest or best part of your day? Is there anything unusual that happened today? Have you heard anything significant, including local and national news events? What was the most inspirational thing you heard today?

TELL THE STORY OF YOUR LIFE IN 10 SENTENCES

Narrate the story of who you are; start with "I am from ...". Try to write your life story in 10 sentences or less.

IMAGINE A BEAUTIFUL CENTURY-OLD TREE...

Which of your neighborhood's trees is the oldest? What has it seen? Tell...

A VALUABLE ADVICE

What piece of advice would you give yourself 25 years ago? What happened 15 years ago? Five years ago? What is your most frequently given piece of advice to people your age? Is it the same or different than advice you would give to a younger or older person, and why?

A MOTIVATIONAL QUOTE

Make up a motivational quote or an inspirational phrase based on what you've experienced and learned over the years.

TELL A POWERFUL MEMORY FROM YOUR CHILDHOOD

Pick a strong memory from young adulthood or your childhood, whether happy, moving, sad, scary or completely mundane. Write it down, including the smallest details.

YOUR GREATEST FEARS AND JOYS

Consider your most recent fears and joys, as well as those that define you today. How have you evolved or changed?

TELL ABOUT AN UNUSUAL EVENT

Watch the news and describe an hour in the life of someone to whom something unusual happened.

WHAT CAN'T YOU SEE IN THE PICTURE?

Find a photo and write about what you can't see in it.

ROLE-PLAYING, IMAGINE THAT YOU ARE...

You're on the run from the law. What was your crime? Where are you going?

TALK ABOUT YOUR FAVORITE PARAGRAPH IN A BOOK YOU LIKE

Choose a favorite paragraph from a book and rewrite it in your own words while retaining the original meaning.

IMAGINE THE FUTURE

You awaken to find yourself 100 years in the future. Describe your extraordinary new life.

THAT WONDERFUL THING...

Begin a story with, "I picked it up to take a closer look and..."

A DELICIOUS SMELL

Describe the aroma that is wafting from the kitchen and making your mouth water.

AN UNFORGETTABLE SUNSET

You've never seen a sunset quite like this one. Describe it in such a way that someone would want to be right there with you.

YOUR FAVORITE SONG

Describe your favorite song's music and lyrics in such a way that someone else will want to listen to it right away.

AN INTERESTING DIALOGUE

Place two characters across from each other and record their entire interaction in dialogue.

CHARACTERS AND PERSONALITIES

Create two or three characters based on people in your life, giving them names and personalities. Explain what motivates them.

A LOUDEST SOUND

Describe the loudest sound you can imagine and have a character experience it for the first time.

CHANGE OF OPINION

Choose an ugly object and make a character see it as beautiful. Make them describe the object to someone else in order to persuade them of its beauty.

FACE YOUR FEARS

Make a list of your top five fears. Write a story in which a character is forced to confront one of those fears.

A MISUNDERSTANDING

Describe two people conversing, but make it clear that they are not talking about the same thing, even if they believe they are.

A FUNNY TO-DO LIST

Make a funny to-do list for a teenager on how to attract a boyfriend or girlfriend.

A CHARACTER AND ITS FEATURES

Make a character based on someone in your life you dislike. Now, write about a situation in which they are shown sympathetically despite their flaws.

A DREAM

Describe an interesting, funny, or recurring dream you have had recently.

A DIFFERENT ENDING

Describe a conflict you recall and how it was resolved. Now, write a conclusion that differs from what actually occurred and leaves the reader wanting more.

WRITE ABOUT YOUR CHILDHOOD BEST FRIEND

Can you remember your childhood best friend and some of your activities together? Where did you use to go? How did you bring your imaginations together?

A SUBJECT THAT INTERESTS YOU

Pick a topic you'd like to learn about, such as astrology, botany, sports, or a specific period of history, and write down anything new you've learned about your chosen topic during the day or week.

YOUR FAMILY'S TRADITIONS

What were some of the traditions that your family followed when you were growing up? Do any of those traditions still exist in your family?

REMIND PROMINENT PLACES FROM YOUR CHILDHOOD

Close your eyes and return to some of your favorite childhood haunts: your childhood home, a relative's home, a school, a store, and a park where you used to play. What do you notice as you follow your memories through these places? Do you recall any smells, sounds, textures, colors, or even tastes?

A PECULIAR SIMILARITY

Which of your parents (or another family member) do you most resemble? How do those similarities make you feel? What distinguishes you?

A SIGNIFICANT TURNING POINT IN YOUR LIFE

Describe a watershed moment in your life. Investigate the experience's past, present, and future.

REMEMBER YOUR FAVORITE SONG FROM LONG AGO

What is one of your favorite old songs that brings back memories or feelings? You might not have your original playback device, but you can probably find the song online by searching the title and artist. Make some time to listen to it (perhaps on repeat), and then, while it's still playing or in silence afterward, explore the memories and feelings that arise. Allow them to dance onto your page to their own beat.

AN INSPIRING EXPERIENCE

Can you recall a conversation or interaction that influenced you? Try to bring your imagination back to that experience and write about it from that place of inspiration.

WHAT MAKES YOU FEEL GOOD

Make a list of three things you do on a regular basis that are good for your health. Describe how each one helps you.

DESCRIBE SOMETHING IMPORTANT TO YOU

Choose something meaningful to you. It could be anything from a treasured relationship to a memento from a memorable trip. Begin by writing about it, and then see where your thoughts naturally lead you.

WRITE ABOUT HISTORICAL FICTION

Choose a historical period or event that interests you. Study it and learn about the people, events, and ideas that defined it.

Then write a fictional work that uses a fictional protagonist and fictional narrative to explore the real concepts of the story.

WRITE A BIOGRAPHY

Choose one person to interview. This could be a family member, friend, or community member. Learn about his or her life and experiences, and then write a literary biography about your subject.

WRITE A MYSTERIOUS SHORT STORY

A stranger offers your character money to transport a mysterious package onto the plane at the airport. The stranger assures your character that nothing is illegal and that everything has already been screened. Your character is wary, but he needs the money, so he agrees...

INDULGE IN A HOBBY (OR MORE)

"To Be Happy In Life, Develop At Least Four Hobbies:
One To Bring You Money, One To Keep You Healthy,
One To Bring You Joy,
And One To Bring You Peace."

-Stan Jacobs-

Hobbies provide you with something interesting and enjoyable to do on your own or as part of a group. Expand on hobbies you enjoyed while working or explore new interests. Wes Moss discovered that the happiest retirees regularly engaged in three to four hobbies.

ADVANTAGES OF HOBBIES

There are so many benefits to having one (or more) hobbies! Here are just a few examples:

- Hobbies can help you build stronger relationships by allowing you to collaborate, share, teach, and learn from and with others.

- Hobbies contribute to your being an interesting, well-rounded individual who others enjoy being around and conversing with.

- Hobbies can help you reduce stress and are great for relaxation. Hobbies are great self-care activities!

- Hobbies are great for your mental health.

- Hobbies can offer you interesting challenges. Overcoming these challenges can boost your confidence and self-esteem.

- Hobbies are ideal for helping you learn new skills, which can lead to growth in lots of areas of your life.

- Hobbies can help improve your memory, focus, and concentration.

- Hobbies can help improve your hand-eye coordination and fine motor skills.

- Hobbies are just fun, plain, and simple!

TYPES OF HOBBIES

The possibilities are endless, and there are numerous types of hobbies available, and everyone will most likely have a favorite category or two.

I'm focusing on eight different categories, or hobby types, for the purposes of this list: physical and active hobbies, creative and DIY craft hobbies, mental hobbies, musical hobbies, collecting hobbies, food and drink hobbies, games and puzzles hobbies, and model or woodworking hobbies. However, here is a selection of ideas that may be of interest to you.

PHYSICAL AND ACTIVE HOBBIES

Sports and other activities that require you to move your body are examples of physical hobbies.

They are beneficial to your physical, mental, and social well-being. You can do some of these things on your own, or you can join local club teams or Facebook groups to meet others.

Best of all, you don't have to be a great athlete to participate in one of these! The goal is to have fun while staying active and improving your skill set. That's all! Here are some fun physical activities to try:

- **Archery**

- **Badminton**

- Barre
- Baseball
- Basketball
- Board games
- Bowling
- Bowling
- Boxing
- Brewery games
- Cheerleading
- Cross country
- Cycling
- Dancing
- Darts
- Fencing
- Figure skating
- Fishing
- Football
- Gardening
- Golf
- Gymnastics
- Hiking

- Horseback riding
- Horse racing
- Ice hockey
- Ice skating
- Jazzercise/aerobics
- Jet skiing
- Juggling
- Karate
- Kickboxing
- Pilates
- Rock climbing
- Roller skating
- Rugby
- Running
- Running track
- Sailing
- Scuba diving
- Skateboarding
- Skiing
- Sky diving
- Snowboarding

- Soccer

- Stretching

- Surfing

- Swimming

- Table tennis

- Taekwondo

- Tai chi

- Tennis

- **Visiting and walking around area gardens**

- Volleyball

- **Walking** (you can walk alone, with your kids, and with friends for activity and fresh air)

- **Water skiing**

- **Weight lifting**

- **Windsurfing**

- **Yoga**

CREATIVE AND DIY CRAFT HOBBIES

Arts and crafts are examples of creative hobbies.

These creative hobbies are great for self-care and alone time, but many of them also have a lot of community and support.

If you're interested in one, you can also look for classes or tips online or at your local recreation center.

If you're really into your hobby, it could also be a great small business! Consider starting a blog or creating a YouTube channel to help you turn your hobby into a profitable business.

Here are some creative hobby ideas for you to try:

- **Acrylic painting**

- **Acting**

- **Building dollhouses**

- **Bullet journaling**

- **Calligraphy**

- **Candle making**

- **Canvas art** (to display handmade art in your home or give some as gifts, too)

- **Card making**

- **Carving**

- **Clay crafts**

- **Collage**

- **Collage making**

- Coloring

- Computer hobbies

- Cricut/silhouette crafts

- Crochet

- Cross stitch

- Designing clothes

- **Designing free printables** (you can create logos, notecards, tote bags, and so much more…)

- Designing graphics

- Diamond painting kit

- Doodling

- Drawing

- Embroidery

- Fashion design

- Fashion photography

- Felt arts

- Floral design

- Flower pressing

- Flower pressing

- Glass blowing

- Glass painting

- Going to museums
- Growing bonsai
- Hair styling
- Hand lettering
- Home decorating
- Jewelry making
- Knitting
- Leather crafts
- Magic
- Makeup art
- Making dolls
- Making dream catchers
- Metal detecting
- Miniatures
- Mod podge crafts
- Nail art
- Oil painting
- Origami
- Paint by number
- Painting rocks
- Party planning

- Pastels

- Photography

- Plan unique date night ideas with your significant other

- Poetry writing

- Pottery/ceramics

- Preserving florals and stems, such as eucalyptus drying

- Printmaking

- Prose writing

- Puppetry

- Quilling

- Quilting

- Rock tumbling

- **Scrapbooking** (an easy-to-begin hobby that also is very satisfying when you're done!)

- Sculpture

- Sewing

- **Sketching** (sketching and doodling are both extremely versatile hobbies. Make them in a sketchbook, make cards to sell on sites like Etsy, or doodle in your planner or bullet journal to unwind!)

- Small space gardening

- **Soap making and soap packaging** (this is an inexpensive hobby that also yields lots of yummy-smelling potential gifts!)

- **Stained glass**

- **Star gazing**

- **Starting a YouTube channel**

- **Sticker collecting**

- **String art**

- **Tie dye**

- **Tissue paper crafts**

- **Upcycled art**

- **Watercolor painting** (painting is so relaxing, and if you take a course or workshop, it also becomes a great social activity)

- **Wood burning**

- **Wreath making**

MENTAL HOBBIES

Hobbies in this category are excellent brain boosters!

They may make you smarter and even help to prevent cognitive decline.

Most of these can be completed alone, but some lend themselves well to group efforts (such as learning a new language by taking a class or traveling with a group of friends).

Mental hobbies can also help you become a smarter, more well-rounded individual. Here are some of my favorite mental pastimes:

- **Blogging**

- **Book club**

- Brain teasers

- Creating a podcast

- Crossword puzzles

- Decorating a planner or happy planner

- Doing puzzles

- Journaling

- **Learning a new language** (languages are a challenging but very rewarding hobby idea)

- **Listening to podcasts**

- **Note-taking and research**

- **Online classes**

- **Quote collecting**

- **Reading** (it's a great hobby for relaxation and self-care, as well as a wonderful educational hobby to learn new skills or information)

- **Start a gratitude list**

- **Starting a blog to educate the public on a specific topic**

- Sudoku

- Travel and travel planning

- Volunteering

- Word scrambles

- Word search and word games

- Writing

MUSICAL HOBBIES

Musical hobbies are extremely popular, and with good reason! They're ideal for stress relief, community building, and learning a new skill.

Here are some great places to start if you want to pursue a musical hobby:

- **Concert or choir photography**

- **Dancing**

- **Joining a band**

- **Joining a choir**

- **Learn to write lyrics**

- **Learning about various musicians/music genres**

- **Learning how to read music**

- **Learning to play cello**

- **Learning to play guitar** (classical, bass, or electric guitar)

- **Learning to play drums**

- **Learning to play keyboard or piano** (If this is a hobby you are interested in, there are many online classes/videos available. That apply to the majority of the musical hobbies on this list!)

- **Learning to play trumpet**

- **Learning to play violin**

- **Listening to music**

- **Memorizing music lyrics**

- **Singing (solo)**

- **Start a music blog**

COLLECTING HOBBIES

Collecting an item or group of items is a fun, relaxing, and low-pressure hobby that you can work on slowly.

If you include learning about and cataloging the items you collect, you can turn your hobby into a wonderful brain-enhancing activity as well!

And having several collections is not only fun, but it can make it easier for friends and family to give you gifts!

Here are some collecting hobbies you might enjoy:

- **Animal-themed items** (example: things related to chipmunks)

- **Art from around the world**

- **Art or coffee table books**

- **Autographed pictures or other items**

- **Baseball cards**

- **Bells**

- **Bird books or items bird-themed**

- **Birdhouses**

- **Books of matches** (this is a popular collection that doesn't take up much space and serves as a great reminder of favorite restaurants you've visited.)

- **Bottle caps**

- **Boy scouts or girl scouts memorabilia**

- Butterfly art or items

- Cake pans

- **Calendars** (framing favorite calendar pages is an excellent way to use your collection as art on a wall. You could even make an entire gallery wall out of your favorite pages!)

- **Candles**

- **Candles**

- **Candlesticks**

- **China patterns**

- **Christmas art and decor**

- **Coasters**

- **Collecting coffee mugs**

- **Collecting tea cups**

- **Collecting teas**

- **Cookbooks**

- **Corks**

- **Cupcake wrappers**

- **Cupcake/muffin pans**

- **Custom pins**

- **Depression glass**

- **Dollhouses**

- **Dolls**

- Driftwood

- Driftwood

- DVDs or VHS tapes

- Figurines

- Fruit-themed decor and items

- Harry potter-themed items (or another book)

- Hats

- Hello Kitty items or collectibles

- Holiday books (collecting and displaying books ahead of a holiday is a great way to get into the spirit)

- Items related to a cartoon, television show, or movie

- Kawai or Japanese items or collectibles

- Kitschy artwork or collectibles

- Ladybug art or items

- Lego sets

- Magnets

- Mason jars (especially vintage)

- Matchbox cards

- Memorabilia from a specific decade

- Mirrors

- Model cars

- Musical instruments

- Nautical or beach-inspired art or items

- Painted/decorated rocks

- Pez dispensers

- **Plants** (plants are a fun, higher maintenance, collection that also double as home and porch décor)

- Postcards

- Presidential memorabilia

- Puzzles

- Records

- Red shoe/high heel/glamour items

- Religious memorabilia

- Rug beaters

- Rum, whiskey, bourbon, or other spirits

- Scarves

- Sea shells

- Sheet music

- Shoes

- Snow-themed items

- Snow globes

- **Specific colorful items** (for example, things that are green)

- Spices from around the world

- Spirit bottles

- Sporting event tickets

- Sports balls or equipment

- Sportsbooks

- Sports jerseys or other memorabilia

- Stamp collecting

- Stuffed animals

- Ties

- Travel books

- Travel brochures

- **T-shirts** (do you have a large collection of t-shirts lying around? Consider having them made into a T-shirt quilt, a warm and cozy way to show off your collection!)

- Unusual or hard to find candy

- Vases or ceramics

- Video games

- Vintage bottles

- Vintage glass

- Vintage milk glass

- Vintage Pyrex

- Vintage spools of thread or sewing notions

- Wine

FOOD AND DRINK HOBBIES

Food and drink hobbies can be pursued alone, but they also work well as a hobby where you can meet new people.

- **Baking**

- **BBQ or grilling**

- **Cocktails**

- **Collect cookbooks or cooking magazines**

- **Collect cooking-related items such as tea cups, dessert plates, mugs, and china patterns... there are numerous places to find unique and fun cooking-related items.**

- **Collect food-related items such as unique teas, spices, and coffees**

- **Cooking**

- **Create elaborate dessert bars**

- **Host a supper club**

- **Make a recipe each month that combines ingredients from a national food holiday for that month.**

- **Make Neapolitan pizza at home**

- **Start a blog focused on snacks**

- **Start a food or drink blog**

- **Take a cooking class**

- Vegan cooking/baking

- Vegetarian cooking/baking

- Wine, beer, or spirits tasting

WOODWORKING OR MODEL HOBBIES

Many people enjoy creating things with their hands. It's often difficult to work, but seeing the end result can be extremely rewarding. Once you've mastered it, these are great items to sell on Etsy, eBay, or at craft fairs.

Here are some model/woodworking hobbies to experiment with:

- **Building wooden toys**

- **Furniture building** (for example, to begin, consider making a DIY bench)

- **Themed model kits** (example: Lego or Star Wars)

- **Model kits** (cars, trains, airplanes, etc.)

- **Wood carving**

- **Wood burning**

- **Wooden-toys**

- **Woodturning**

GAMES AND PUZZLES HOBBIES

A hobby list would be incomplete without a section on games and puzzles!

Games and puzzles are examples of hobbies that are ideal for the cooler fall and winter months.

Do these online, at home with your friends, or with family for a hobby that can be tailored to your preferences, whether you want to practice self-care or make new friends and meet new people!

Here are some game hobbies to try:

- **3D puzzles**

- **Bingo**

- **Card games**

- **Checkers**

- **Chess**

- **Theme-based games** (Fortnite Printables or Harry Potter Party Games, for example)

- **Online games**

- **Lawn games**

- **Other board games**

- **Puzzles**

- **Sudoku**

- **Video games**

- **Word games and puzzles**

Get an Education

"Develop A Passion For Learning.
If You Do, You Will Never Cease To Grow."

-Anthony J. D'Angelo-

GET A DEGREE

Retirement may be the ideal time to pursue that degree you've always wanted or simply learn more about a subject that interests you. Every state provides free or reduced college tuition for older adults, though the age requirements vary.

LEARNING PROGRAMS

If you're more interested in gaining knowledge than formal credentials, you might want to look into one of the Bernard Osher Foundation's lifelong learning programs. Programs for adults over the age of 50 are available at colleges and universities across the country. Courses are reasonably priced (some as low as $35), but they do not provide college credit.

Furthermore, there are numerous free ways to broaden your mind without spending any money.

VISIT SCIENCE CENTERS AND MUSEUMS

Many offer free admission on specific days or for seniors in general.

LISTEN TO A PODCAST OR TED TALK

MASSIVE OPEN ONLINE COURSES (MOOCS)

Provide free college-level training in a wide range of subjects such as web design, game development, communication, chemistry, music, art, economics, psychology, and others.

START A SMALL BUSINESS

You can create and market whatever good or service you want now that you aren't worried about making a living. Many retirees use their years of knowledge to work as independent consultants or advisors. You might also think about earning more money by:

ACADEMIC COACH

Tutoring is a logical step after teaching because it enables you to keep improving the lives of those who require extracurricular academic support or help with college preparation.

SENIOR DAY CARE

Adult daycare organizations offer a place and activities for elders to enjoy throughout the day rather than serving as residential communities.

RESIDENTIAL CARE FACILITY

Nursing homes and assisted living facilities offer comparable services on a slightly different scale. Residents have a little more freedom, but they still have access to staff who can assist with tasks and provide medical care.

USING AN ATM

You run this kind of business by deploying ATMs in busy areas and earning money for each withdrawal that is made.

INFANT CHILDCARE FACILITY

Young parents may find it challenging to balance work and child care. As a result, people constantly look for daycare facilities; why don't you think about opening one? It will give them a sense of security to leave their child with an experienced caregiver. The knowledge, warmth, and love their child receives will also be treasured forever!

CHILDCARE SERVICES

Did you know that studies have shown that younger children and older individuals can support one another emotionally? Profit from this and offer your spare time to watch children for others.

GARDEN NURSERY

Take note, gardeners with a backyard and spare time. Depending on your space and ambition, growing and selling trees and shrubs from your own house is a terrific opportunity to make an extra few thousand dollars a year or even every month.

BECOME AN ONLINE ASSISTANT

To save costs, a lot of small business owners and entrepreneurs use virtual assistants. From their homes, virtual assistants can plan meetings or projects, make phone calls, enter data, construct spreadsheets, or even assist with writing or graphic design work.

MAKE AN ANGEL INVESTMENT

You've put a lot of effort into your career and prospered on your own. You don't have a problem with money; in fact, you have more of it than you know what to do with. You adore the thought of assisting someone in going mainstream with their enthusiasm. As it succeeds, they'll even pay you big royalties!

OWNER OF A BED AND BREAKFAST

If you have a reputation for providing exceptional service and have been dubbed the host or hostess with the mostest, you may have what it takes to run a prosperous bed and breakfast.

BLOGGING

People use the internet to find entertainment and information. If you can use your site to give them what they're looking for, you can monetize it in many other ways, including affiliate marketing.

SERVICE FOR BUSINESS PLANS

Did you know that only 33% of newly established business owners polled had a formal business plan? There is a huge market opportunity for a business plan service, given that there are about 28 million small enterprises in the United States. You should be familiar with business planning, be able to undertake the necessary research and be able to run the necessary calculations before beginning such a service.

PURCHASE A COMPANY

Starting a business from scratch is no simple undertaking. If you don't want to spend years working to build your business, you might be better suited purchasing one that already has some customers. When you contemplate the potential for instant gains, if you have the financial means to accomplish so, it can possibly be the more advantageous course of action!

GET A COFFEE CART FOR SALE OR RENT

The Specialty Coffee Association of America estimates that specialty coffee products provide gross revenues of between 55.1% and 61.51% per cup. Purchase or hire an espresso cart, then visit local athletic events, concerts, and farmer's markets.

Buy to sell Look for excellent deals on vintage clothing, furniture, toys, and other collectibles at flea markets, estate sales, and garage sales. To sell your antiques, you can set up a booth at weekend fairs or rent space from antique cooperatives.

BAKERY OF CAKES AND CUPCAKES

The creation, decoration, and sale of unique cakes and cupcakes for events such as birthdays, weddings, and anniversaries is a terrific business venture for the home baker to explore and has the potential to be very successful.

BUSINESS OF PRODUCING CANDLES

Since more individuals are spending time at home and want to create a peaceful atmosphere, candle-making is making a comeback in the market. Before you start selling candles, learn how to produce them and add your own creative spin.

CATERING COMPANY

Do you enjoy preparing meals for your friends and family? Why not start a catering company using your passion for food? Offering modest meal trays for order is a good place to start, and as you gain expertise and equipment, you may expand to managing dinner events and larger parties.

RETAIL CLOTHING BRANDS

Do you enjoy wearing clothes and fashion? Do you enjoy shopping for clothing at sales and secondhand stores? Why not start a clothing buy and sell business? You may influence a lot more people with your passion for fashion by spending money on the companies and trends you enjoy.

WRITING CONTENT

For online product and service promotion, brands rely heavily on high-quality content. Numerous specialized companies assist brands in producing content on any subject imaginable. You can start working as a content writer if you believe you are proficient in the language they need the information written in and have excellent research skills. Join online writing services like Elance, Freelancer, Upwork, or Peopleperhour to get started straight away.

COPYWRITING

A copywriting business may be the ideal way for you to make money if you have a knack for writing in a clear and concise style that will pique readers' and viewers' interest and inspire them to do the required action. Copywriters create text or copy for publications such as press releases, catalogs, package labels, websites, advertising, and print and online marketing materials.

CRAFTS STUDIO

This is a laid-back and comforting business concept. It enables you to keep doing the crafts and arts you adore while earning money from them by teaching others how to do them. It's simple to organize informal workshops at your home or at the neighborhood community center, but thanks to modern technology, doing it remotely via video chat programs like Zoom is now even simpler.

INNOVATIVE ITEMS

Do you have a knack for making things? You might be a talented artist or a skillful quilter. If so, you might be able to make some additional money by selling your artistic creations.

CONSUMER ASSISTANCE

Everything can now be done online due to the widespread use of the internet. Consider creating an electronic customer service business where you can offer to handle the online customer service requirements of other businesses and brands if you enjoy talking to people and have outstanding problem-solving abilities. This may involve responding to questions and taking orders by email, Facebook, live chat, or the phone.

STUDIO FOR DANCE

Not only is dancing a fantastic kind of fitness, but it's also a lot of fun! Why not convert some excess space in your home into a dance studio if you enjoy dancing? You may rent it out or even have events like dance classes there.

SERVICE OF DELIVERY

You can provide a delivery service where you bring seniors who don't want to run their own errands stuff like food and groceries.

MAKE UNIQUE JEWELRY AND ACCESSORIES

Use your artistic skills to design unique jewelry and accessories. Art exhibits, craft fairs, and holiday boutiques are good places to sell your unique earrings, pins, bracelets, necklaces, and belt buckles.

MAKING CLOTHES

Making and selling cloth diapers, duvets, plush animals, pet outfits, bed linens, and pillowcases are some things you might do with your sewing talents.

GOODS ON DROPSHIP

Dropshipping is a type of internet business that often operates as a sole proprietorship and sells goods to clients without actually keeping any inventory. You are in charge of building a website, deciding which goods to offer, marketing those goods, and setting prices. When a consumer places an order on your website, you submit the order to a dropshipping supplier, who prepares it and ships it to the customer.

EBAY/AMAZON/ETSY/ECOMMERCE

You undoubtedly have a lot of items around the house that you don't want or need any more after years of working and raising a family. By selling your worn and unwanted stuff on eBay or Craigslist, you can make money.

eBooks If you enjoy writing but find blogging to be uninteresting, consider writing eBooks. Why not share your incredible tales with the world while earning money in the process?

EVENT COORDINATOR

Professional event planning, which is expected to expand by 18% between 2020 and 2030, is a growing industry that makes a fantastic second career for people with perfect attention to detail and unwavering inventiveness.

FRANCHISEE

In the world of franchise business ownership, there is something for everyone, with approximately 760,000 franchise businesses generating approximately $760 billion in revenue in the United States.

GARAGE AND ATTIC CLEANING AND HAULING

Nobody wants to spend a weekend cleaning out the garage, attic, or garden shed; it's dirty and time-consuming, and when you're finished, you still have to cart away all that discarded rubbish. Cleaning and transportation services might be profitable.

IN-HOME GENERAL CARE

Many elders might benefit from non-medical professionals visiting on a regular basis to assist with various household activities such as laundry, cooking, and errand running.

TRANSPORTATION IN GENERAL

Many elders opt not to drive at all or are unable to owe to medical concerns. So you might also start a general transportation service aimed at seniors who want assistance running errands or getting out of the house.

HANDYMAN

Handyman services, such as painting and minor repairs, furniture assembly, and lighting installation are always in high demand. If you are handy, you can make money from homeowners, seniors, and others who do not want to fix it themselves. Advertise in consumer magazines and on bulletin boards, and leave leaflets at real estate offices. Then begin mending everything from broken windows to leaking faucets.

SERVICES FOR HEALTH AND FITNESS

Maintaining good health and fitness is essential at any age. However, as we become older, it becomes even more important to take care of our health. You can turn your passion for health and fitness into a company by becoming a fitness guru if you've spent your life practicing wellness activities like yoga or pilates or if you're basically an authority on multivitamins and superfoods.

Home Improvements Some older homeowners may benefit from home improvements as they age. If you're a talented home remodeler, you may provide a service in which you put safety bars in bathrooms, redesign corridors to accommodate wheelchairs, or even construct automated lifts around staircases.

ALTERATION SERVICE AT HOME

It's time to leverage on your skills and ideas by offering garment and fabric modification services from the comfort of your own home, and earn a lot of money in the process.

CLEANING THE HOUSE

If you wish to specialize in a specific home-based service, you can provide weekly or monthly house cleaning visits to seniors who are unable to complete certain tasks in their homes.

HOUSE KEEPING

You can assist other elders by watching over their home and/or pets while they are away, giving them peace of mind.

MEDICAL CARE AT HOME

Many elderly choose to remain in their own homes but could benefit from frequent medical treatment. A nurse or medical expert would visit on a regular basis to deliver medication and related forms of care with this type of service.

INVESTMENT ADVISOR

If you have excellent investment knowledge, you can advise them on stock markets, mutual funds, SIPs, and other investment options. For starters, your major clientele could be older people who want to handle their spare money.

LANDLORD

Simply said, real estate is a good investment. It has always been, and it most likely always will be.

LANDSCAPING

Another area where many elders could benefit from assistance is landscaping. Provide general lawn mowing, gardening, or even more advanced landscape design services to seniors in your area so they can keep their outdoor space in good condition.

PLANTS FOR RENT

If you've always had a green thumb, you may consider reaching out to the large network of businesses and homeowners that lease plants rather than owning them. In this business concept, you choose appropriate plants for various places and charge a monthly fee for watering, pruning, and responding to plant crises.

Make YouTube videos If you wish to make videos, you can create a YouTube channel. There are many really successful YouTubers in their latter years. The older age provides some wonderful information on this site, ranging from gardening, cooking, and knitting to personal finance and investing.

ASSISTANCE WITH MEDICAL CLAIMS

People of all ages may find it challenging to manage the health insurance claims process. However, it is especially important for elders who may require extensive care. By offering this service, you would assist senior clients in filing claims and determining the best course of action for their health insurance.

TRANSCRIPTION OF MEDICAL DOCUMENTS

Work as a vital member of a medical team from the comfort of your own home. Hospitals, doctors, dentists, chiropractors, and veterinarians are in high demand for aid in transcribing patient medical records. Medical terminology and linguistic skills training helps keep your company running smoothly.

MENTORING PROGRAM

There is wisdom and insight that only age can provide. If you believe you have much to share and contribute, you might begin offering your mentorship and life coaching services to younger people who still require guidance in their lives.

MOBILE SALON

If elderly people require assistance with their hair, nails, or other salon services but are unwilling to leave their homes, you might start a mobile salon and provide such services to them.

MANAGING YOUR MONEY

Many seniors are on limited incomes or are about to retire, which means they could benefit from financial advice.

MUSIC INSTRUCTION

What are you waiting for if you can teach people to sing, play guitar, piano, drums, or a wind or string instrument? Profit from your skills and earn a good full- or part-time income by teaching others how to play your instrument of choice. Classes can be held one-on-one or in a group setting, in your home, the student's home, a rented commercial space, or a community center, in collaboration with community programmers, continuing education, or a well-established music store.

MARKETING VIA A NETWORK

Network marketing, like retail, can be done online or locally in your own neighborhood. Choose a reputable brand or company whose products you believe in and like, and urge others to buy and sell them as well. Because this business relies on your social skills and network, it should be a fantastic business option if you've spent years refining those.

MEDICAL TRANSPORTATION FOR NON-EMERGENCY SITUATIONS

If you want to start a transportation business, many seniors could benefit from assistance traveling to regular doctor appointments or other appointments where they may not be able to drive themselves.

NURSING FACILITY

A nursing home is an institution that provides medical care to older people around the clock. Some specialize in treating certain disorders, such as dementia, while others are more general.

NUTRITIONAL ADVICE

People of all ages require proper nutrition. It is especially important for elders. Provide consultancy services in which you assist elderly customers in developing meal plans and staying healthy.

HOME AND OFFICE ORGANIZER

Help pack rats, overburdened CEOs, and other organizationally challenged people clear out cluttered closets, straighten papers, and get rid of the extra clutter.

ONLINE CLASSES

By 2024, the online learning/training market is estimated to approach $200 billion. If you have a skill that others would pay to acquire and are skilled at expressing things, you may tap into that market by converting your knowledge into one or more online courses.

JURORS ON THE INTERNET

Even if they never attended law school or the police academy, retired folks can put on their real-life crime sleuthing hats. They can even work as jurors without leaving their homes. Companies like eJury, Online Verdict, and Jury Test pay people to sit on mock juries and provide comments on cases handled by attorneys and other jury consultants.

ONLINE INVESTIGATOR

Consider beginning an internet research business if you enjoy digging for information or miss spending hours at the library working on academic papers and want to augment your income. It's a terrific way to get paid for your time spent reading and perusing the web!

PAINTING LESSONS

Do you enjoy painting and art? You can begin by teaching painting classes and creating a home painting studio. This is a fantastic company that not only capitalizes on your own interests and skills but also serves to promote artistic beauty to others around you. Once you've built a following, you might consider opening a gallery or a small store where you can sell your paintings and teach classes.

SENIOR PARTY PLANNING

Why not cater to your specific neighborhood if you enjoy hosting and creating parties? As a senior, you understand your peers' demands and desires, whether they arrange a get-together or throw a little party. Use this expertise to become the best party planner in your neighborhood.

PATIENT REPRESENTATIVE

Those dealing with personal or family medical issues will benefit from the assistance and understanding of a patient advocate, who can assist them in understanding and navigating health and care-related decisions, as well as insurance and billing issues.

CHEF ON STAFF

Prepare home-cooked meals for busy professionals and working parents who employ you as a personal chef.

PERSONAL ASSISTANT

If you enjoy shopping, this is the business for you. Start a personal shopping service to help those who are too busy to shop, don't like to shop, or can't get out to do their own shopping and make a lot of money.

PET SITTING OR PET CARE

Seniors who have dogs may require assistance walking or grooming them on a regular basis. Consider launching a business where you can spend all day cuddling with your customers.

PHOTOGRAPHER

Photography is a passion that can quickly transform into a lucrative and gratifying small company with a good eye and the correct equipment.

FRAMER OF PHOTOGRAPHS

Use a picture framing business to put yourself in the frame. You can collaborate with gallery owners, artists, portrait photographers, and those who have purchased a print, painting, or great photograph.

PLANT LEASING AND UPKEEP

If you have a green thumb and a delivery vehicle, you might provide fresh greenery to firms, home builders, fitness clubs, and other enterprises. Regular watering, pruning, and fertilizing are among the services provided.

PRODUCTS THAT MAKE EVERYDAY LIFE EASIER

A button poke, click, swipe, or voice command can be used to activate technological gadgets. However, many people (particularly the elderly) require assistance in setting up and learning how to use these gadgets, creating a business potential for you.

CONSULTANT ON PROJECTS

Your professional views, expertise, and perspective are valuable assets for individuals who have polished particular skills and sets of information over years of experience.

PROPERTY ADVISOR

When consumers invest in real estate or insurance, they require assurance and sound guidance. Unfortunately, with a concentration on fulfilling financial targets, these two qualities are becoming increasingly difficult to locate. If you provide consistent service, your name will swiftly spread through word-of-mouth, eventually leading to major business growth.

SPEAKING IN PUBLIC

Another alternative is to become a public speaker and share your knowledge and views with the next generation.

RAMP CONSTRUCTION

Ramps can also be used around the outside of senior houses. This is a rather simple service that you can provide by collaborating with ramp suppliers in your area.

RETIREMENT RESIDENCE

Retirement communities are mostly residential facilities rather than medical institutions. They offer senior-friendly living options and may even organize special activities to keep residents engaged.

JOBS IN RV/CAMPING

Many people regard retirement as the perfect moment to ditch their commuting automobiles in favor of RVs. Almost 9% of US households headed by someone over the age of 55 own an RV, and with gas prices rising, these new road hogs surely wouldn't mind making a buck or two while rolling across the country. Campgrounds frequently offer RVers a range of short-term jobs, such as front desk work, security detail, grounds keeping, maintenance, housekeeping, and rentals, in exchange for free rooms, water hookups, and other advantages.

OFFER HOMEMADE CUISINE FOR SALE.

Are you adept at baking or preparing pickles and party foods like biryani? If so, begin by accepting small orders from your neighbors. If you provide an excellent service, this type of business will typically grow organically and swiftly. Furthermore, there is a growing desire for organic and healthy food, so start preparing some of your recipes and get started!

CONSULTING FOR SENIORS

You can also assist families in sorting through the various possibilities that come with aging. You can assist them in locating nursing homes or retirement communities and navigating the process of receiving suitable care.

SENIOR FITNESS CLASSES

If you want to start a fitness business, you can provide programs or personal training sessions tailored exclusively to elders.

RELOCATING SENIORS

You can offer moving aid to seniors who are getting ready to move into retirement communities or just downsizing into a smaller area, covering everything from packing to selling or giving certain possessions.

SENIORS AND SMART TECHNOLOGY

They claim smart technology is reserved for the technologically savvy. Guess what: smart home technologies to assist seniors live independently despite deteriorating senses or diminished mobility will benefit seniors far more! Smart home technology such as a whole-house security system, smart smoke detectors, emergency contact systems, smart thermostats, voice-controlled appliances and lights, and a door lock with a video camera are examples of how smart home technology may help seniors live safely and securely. Why not invest in these and begin selling them to your senior friends?

MANUFACTURING OF SOAP

Learning how to manufacture soap is a simple yet fascinating process. In fact, there is a growing trend of making vegan soaps or soaps flavored with actual flowers and fruits. Try starting this business with your own creativity.

AGING IN PLACE CONSULTING IS YOUR SPECIALTY.

As the population ages, many Americans have sought the assistance of specialists to redesign their homes with safety and functionality in mind, as well as provide recommendations on how to live more independently.

SPECIALTY MEDICAL CARE

People are more likely to require healthcare treatments such as physiotherapy, massage therapy, and orthotics. These need particular skills and training, but given today's demographic trends, they are tremendous business potential. Alternative medical treatments such as acupuncture, Chinese medicine, aromatherapy, and naturopathic medicine are becoming more popular.

BEGIN AN ENTERTAINMENT SERVICE REPAIR BUSINESS

Assist homeowners who want to keep their stereo, CD player, or videocassette recorder in working order.

ECO-FRIENDLY AND SUSTAINABLE PRODUCTS

If you want to start a more retail-focused business, look for sustainable and eco-friendly products, which are becoming increasingly popular. Personally, I believe that this is an excellent way to give back to the community because we are contributing to a brighter future for the next generation.

TAXES AND BOOKKEEPING

Many business owners require assistance with bookkeeping. If you worked in accounting or tax preparation during your working life, you might want to consider providing financial consulting services in retirement.

TECHNICAL ASSISTANCE

A large number of seniors use social media, smartphones, and streaming services. However, some people may struggle with cutting-edge technology. So, if you're knowledgeable in these areas, you can help those who need to set up new devices or accounts.

THE TOUR GUIDE

Becoming a private tour guide is an excellent way to stay active while sharing the sights, sounds, and flavors of your favorite places with others who want to learn about them.

TOY DESIGNER

Building and selling children's toys is a great way to make cherished memories for children while also supplementing your income. Consider all of the toys you could create: wooden toys, dollhouses, stuffed animals, dolls, antique toy replicas, and puzzles, to name a few.

SERVICE FOR GROUP TRAVEL

Many seniors choose to travel during their retirement years. Many people may prefer to do so in groups. You can start a travel service that organizes group outings for senior citizens.

DESIGN OF A T-SHIRT

If you're an artist looking for a new medium, design and sell T-shirts. Paint, draw, bead, or appliqué your designs on plain T-shirts, then sell them at farmers' markets, craft fairs, and to your friends and their friends.

CHILDREN'S TUTORING SERVICES

You do not need to be a teacher to take home tuition. All you need is a strong command of a few subjects. Contact the parents in your area and begin tuition classes at your home. When their child is nearby, parents usually feel safe. As your reputation grows, so will your business.

MAKE A HOBBY A BUSINESS

Maybe you're sick of doing the same tasks at work and don't want to turn it into a business. Fortunately, home businesses can also be developed from hobbies. Is your hobby a product or service that you can sell, or can you teach others how to do it through live courses (online or off) or an information product, such as a book or email course? You can start a blog or a podcast and earn money through affiliate marketing and/or advertising.

SERVICE OF VALET PARKING

A driver's license, the ability to obtain third-party liability insurance, and an outgoing, friendly personality are the three requirements for the special-events valet parking service business idea.

ROUTE OF THE VENDING MACHINE

Vending machine routes are a fantastic side business to start. They have low startup costs and do not require constant attention. In contrast to a traditional business, there is no need for someone to "man" the store. All you have to do is run a few routes to replenish inventory and collect your money. This is something you can do on the weekend or in your spare time.

HANGING WALLPAPER

With your wallpaper-hanging skills, you can help residential and commercial clients transform drab walls into works of art. Create a thriving business through excellent referrals and repeat customers. Distribute fliers at paint and wallpaper stores, as well as in shopper publications, homeowner-association newsletters, and bulletin boards at local supermarkets and malls.

MAKE A NEWSLETTER

In recent years, personal email newsletters have grown in popularity. Substack, a startup that allows you to create, distribute, and monetize newsletters, has more than doubled its readership and the total number of newsletters since the COVID-19 pandemic began. The idea is simple: you pick a topic that interests you and that you believe others will enjoy, and you write a newsletter about it. People typically distribute their newsletters for free for a few months to build an audience before transitioning to a subscription model with a monthly fee (typically ranging from $5 to $25 or more). After you monetize, platforms like Substack will take a 10% cut of your revenue.

EDITING AND WRITING

If you have strong communication skills, you may be able to supplement your income by assisting businesses, particularly small businesses, with their communication needs.

YOGA CENTER

Yoga is still practiced by many seniors because it is a beneficial activity for both the mind and the body. If you're one of them, why not invite more retirees to join you by opening a yoga or tai chi studio in your neighborhood?

Being Physically Active

"Exercise Is The Key Not Only To Physical Health But To Peace Of Mind."

-Nelson Mandela-

GET INVOLVED IN A SPORT

Physical activity has a plethora of health benefits, such as improving flexibility, boosting your immune system, and keeping your heart and lungs healthy. Sports are also a great way to meet new people and have fun. Sports popular among retirees include bocce, pickleball, bowling, golf, tennis, and water aerobics. You could join an older adult team or use your athletic ability to coach younger athletes.

And just because you're retired doesn't mean you have to give up serious competition. The National Senior Games Association organizes an Olympic-style competition for people aged 50 and up that includes 20 sports, including cycling, horseshoes, archery, power walking, shuffleboard, volleyball, badminton, and table tennis. Before proceeding to the national games, participants must qualify at the state level.

And for many more ideas on what sports to play, check out the list of Physical and active hobbies.

SET NEW FITNESS GOALS

Even if you're not a sports fan, you can stay fit and active. Participating in a senior exercise class can help you stay on track with your fitness goals. Biking, swimming, and tai chi are all low-impact activities that can help you improve your endurance, strength, flexibility, and balance. Join a gym, train for a marathon, try yoga for seniors or join a walking group.

As an added bonus, being more active during the day will help you sleep better at night.

MENTOR OTHERS

"IF YOUR ACTIONS INSPIRE OTHERS TO DREAM MORE, LEARN MORE, DO MORE, AND BECOME MORE, YOU ARE A LEADER."

-SIMON SINEK-

Sharing your knowledge can be a very rewarding way to give back. Being a mentor to a young person allows you to act as both a teacher and a coach while making a positive difference in the life of a child. Furthermore, research published in The Journals of Gerontology Series A: Biological Sciences and Medical Sciences found that senior adults who mentor young people are three times happier than those who do not. Mentors, according to a Harvard Business Review article, also improve cognitive functioning. Here are a few ways you can help:

EXPERIENCE CORPS

THE NATIONAL MENTORING PARTNERSHIP

BIG BROTHERS BIG SISTERS OF AMERICA

Of course, there are numerous other ways to share your knowledge and experience with others. Teach a class at your neighborhood community center or library. Provide tutoring to high school or college students. Alternatively, you could help local entrepreneurs grow their businesses by volunteering with the SCORE Association.

Join or Start a Club

"The Most Important Things In Life
Are The Connections You Make With Others."

-Tom Ford-

Meeting other people who share your interests is a great way to make new friends and learn new things. Check with your local seniors' center to see what kinds of groups are active in your area, and if you can't find one that focuses on your specific interest, consider starting your own. What are some examples? They are very common clubs that focus on:

- **Amnesty International Club**

- **Art History Club**

- **Books Club**

- **Chess Club**

- **Cooking Club**

- **Creative Writing Club**

- **Dance Club**

- **Films Club**

- **Foreign Language Club**

- **Gardening Club**

- **History Club**

- **Improv Club**

- **Investment Club**

- Mathletes Club

- Medical Professional Club

- Photography Club

- Political Affiliation Clubs

- Pottery Club

- Quilting Club

- Religious Clubs

- Robotic Club

- Soup Kitchen Club

- Video Game Club

- Walking Club

BE SOCIAL

"IN A WORLD OF ALGORITHMS, HASHTAGS, AND FOLLOWERS,
KNOW THE TRUE IMPORTANCE OF HUMAN CONNECTION... "

-UNKNOWN-

Humans are social creatures. You have plenty of time now that you don't have to go to work every day to focus on strengthening your social connections. This is not only enjoyable, but it is also beneficial to your health. According to research published in the American Journal of Epidemiology and Ageing Research Reviews, maintaining strong social ties can improve your overall cognitive health and reduce your risk of developing conditions such as heart disease and dementia.

ARRANGE REGULAR GET-TOGETHERS WITH OTHER RETIREES

ART CLASSES

Retirement can pave the way for newfound creativity for seniors who have worked hard their entire lives just to make a living. Watercolor or acrylic painting, as well as sketching and drawing, are all popular forms of artistic expression; creating art in a group can be a fun way to interact with others.

BOOK CLUBS

If you are a voracious reader, chances are you enjoy the opportunity to share your thoughts on a book with others. Book clubs not only help seniors stay sharp, mentally alert, and in touch with the world, but they also have a large social component.

GARDENING CLUBS

Gardening is an excellent way to get outside while remaining active and connected to others. Digging in the dirt, planting, and weeding can help seniors relax and unwind; they also get to enjoy the fruits of their labor, such as tasty veggies or beautiful flowers.

FIELD TRIPS AND EXCURSIONS

Nobody wants to spend their entire day at home, even if that home is a vibrant assisted living community. The best communities provide special trips and excursions to local attractions such as museums, symphonies, and nature preserves. Some organizations even collaborate with community service organizations to assist seniors in volunteering and giving back.

LECTURES AND CONTINUING ED CLASSES

Increasing one's knowledge base is a surefire way to keep one's mind alert and engaged. Some communities offer on-site lectures or continuing education classes to help with this, while others arrange for residents to take advantage of nearby colleges' academic and cultural offerings.

GROUP EXERCISE CLASSES

Group exercises, such as tai chi, yoga, or Feldenkrais, are enjoyable and social ways to improve balance and flexibility, which are important factors in preventing falls in older adults. Some communities provide chair exercise classes, while others may provide water aerobics programs, which may be appealing to seniors suffering from arthritis.

LIFE STORY EXERCISES

There may be no more meaningful activity for elders than writing down their own unique life story, or gathering photos and mementos in a scrapbook — not only do they preserve a piece of history, but they also get the chance to reflect on their own life experiences.

LIVE MUSIC

Seniors today are members of a generation that revolutionized music. Many people are still sound aficionados with very specific tastes. This interest is catered to in senior living communities by providing live music, including concerts by local artists.

PLAN MOVIE NIGHTS

PLAN WINE-TASTING PARTIES

SPEND QUALITY TIME WITH YOUR GRANDCHILDREN OR OTHER FAMILY MEMBERS

RECONNECT WITH YOUR OLD FRIENDS THROUGH FACEBOOK OR SCHOOL REUNIONS.

SPA DAYS AND SELF-CARE

Everyone understands the value of self-care. Its worth does not end with one's senior years. Spend a very special day at the spa with friends, including a haircut, manicure, or skin treatment to promote wellness.

WALKING CLUBS

Walking around the neighborhood is an easy way for a senior to stay active and can be a good way to meet new people. Some communities even provide transportation for club members to walk in a nearby park or along a walking path.

WII SPORTS

You may not be able to shoot baskets anymore, but Nintendo's Wii inter-active console games, which require you to move your body rather than pressing buttons or using a joystick, provide a fun alternative. Sports-mind-ed seniors can participate in a variety of activities, including bowling, ten-nis, and golf, in addition to the aforementioned basketball.

WORK PART-TIME

Do you want to keep one foot in the workplace? According to the Merrill Lynch survey, nearly 70% of newly retired people work part-time. Many seniors appreciate the opportunity to put their existing skills (or develop new ones) to use while earning a little extra money. You can pursue any field that interests you without having to worry about climbing the corporate ladder. Furthermore, IZA World of Labor research found that people who worked past the age of retirement had high levels of happiness, well-being, and life satisfaction.

Here are some of the best senior part-time jobs.

INDIVIDUAL COACHING

Many retirees and seniors have spent decades learning and training in their fields, and they are in an excellent position to pass that knowledge on and be compensated for it.

ACCOUNTANT

Seniors and retirees with accounting experience may be drawn to this occupation, which has many short-term assignments available across the country for a wide range of employers.

UBER OR LYFT DRIVER

Driving is a good part-time job for retirees because they can set their own schedules and have more daytime flexibility during the day than the average 9-to-5 employee. One possibility is to become an Uber or Lyft driver.

DELIVERIES

Postmates and Shipt are two companies to look into for part-time delivery jobs for seniors and retirees. Other types of driver and delivery jobs are available on FlexJobs, including pharmacy deliveries.

If you don't feel comfortable driving people for Uber, you might prefer driving food for Uber Eats. It is one of several companies that hire food delivery drivers. Another example is Instacart, a grocery shopping, and delivery service.

DOG WALKING AND PET SITTING

Dog walking is especially beneficial for people over 50:

- Flexible scheduling

- Control over your business

- Extra income

Check out these nationwide companies to see if you have what it takes to be Fido-friendly: Rover, Wag, and Barkly Pets. You can sign up for pet care, housekeeping, senior care, and child care at Care.com.

CONCIERGE

Older residents can help hotel guests find good restaurants, family attractions, and other activities by using their extensive knowledge of their city.

Concierge jobs for seniors and retirees are also available at resorts in high-demand areas such as Florida and Arizona, where snowbirds flock during the cold-weather months.

HOLIDAY JOBS

Long lines of shoppers, fitting rooms strewn with tried-on clothes, and a flurry of inventory work accompany the holidays. Cashiers, sales associates, and customer service representatives are typically in high demand by retailers during the hectic weeks between Thanksgiving and Christmas. This is an excellent option for retirees seeking part-time excitement and end-of-year cash. Amazon, Kohl's, Michael's, and Target are among the retailers that traditionally hire a large number of new employees for the holiday season.

NATIONAL PARK SERVICE JOBS

Seasonal job openings at the National Park Service include positions as a ranger or park guide for a few months each year. Aramark, which manages resorts, recreational activities, and lodges in several state and national parks and scenic destinations across the United States, has many opportunities for seasonal and part-time workers.

CONSULTING

This part-time job, providing expert advice to businesses, is one of the most lucrative part-time jobs for seniors and retirees, allowing them to put their decades of experience to good use. To become a consultant, you do not need an Ivy League MBA. If you have extensive knowledge and training in your field, a company may be willing to pay for it. Consulting jobs are among the most popular jobs that can be done from home. Udemy and Become are two companies that show would-be consultants the first steps or provide training.

BLOGGER

Websites such as ElderChicks, Senior Planet, and The Senior Nomads debunk the myth that seniors don't do technology. Consider starting a blog or a video blog (also known as a "vlog") if you have visual creativity, a way with words, and a lot of great stories and ideas to share. Tips and tricks can be found in Blogging Basics 101 and ProBlogger.

SPORTS COACH

We have athletes of all shapes and sizes competing in every sport imaginable, and many seniors share their sporting passions by working with children at schools, community centers, and youth sports organizations.

MENTOR COACH

Many young entrepreneurs and professionals have a lot of energy, ambition, and ideas, but they need someone with experience to help mold all of that into success and avoid costly pitfalls.

Seniors and retirees who have built their own businesses can become professional trainers. Alternatively, you could volunteer to assist early-stage entrepreneurs.

PERSONAL ASSISTANT

These professionals handle mundane tasks so that their bosses can concentrate on high-level projects without becoming bogged down. Screening calls, returning emails, running errands, and scheduling appointments are all examples of duties. This can be a desirable job for retirees and seniors because it offers flexible hours and decent pay without the stress of stressful responsibility.

TRANSLATOR OR INTERPRETER

Translators and interpreters are more needed than ever in our increasingly multilingual world, including government offices, social service agencies, and customer service centers.

Bilingual and multilingual seniors and retirees who have become certified can choose from a wide range of options.

SUBSTITUTE TEACHING

As substitutes, senior and retired teachers can bring a lifetime of experience, knowledge, and training to the classroom. They know how to manage a room full of curious, energetic, and sometimes rowdy children who are often fascinated by the new adult in the room.

According to the National Education Association, depending on where you live, you may or may not require a teaching license or a substitute teaching license. You will almost certainly need a bachelor's degree.

SECURITY GUARD

Maybe you used to be a cop or served in the military and gained policing experience.

Those are excellent credentials if you want to supplement your income as a security guard. These jobs aren't always in a mall or a bank. Security is used in the following industries:

- Health care

- Construction

- Ports

- Mining

- Condominium management

- Business

Security Guard Training HQ is a good place to start learning about training and job opportunities across the country.

GOLF COURSE MARSHAL OR RANGER

After spending a lot of time on golf courses over the years, seniors and retirees may enjoy the idea of giving back to the sport while also making some money.

Golf course marshals keep fans quiet during players' shots, search for stray balls, assist spectators, and generally ensure that everything runs smoothly throughout the course.

Indeed and ZipRecruiter are good places to look for a golf course "marshal" or "ranger" jobs.

TAX PREPARERS

This is an excellent job for retirees due to the seasonal nature of tax season (roughly December until Tax Day). You can spend the summer and early fall months with family and on vacation and then earn extra money during the dark, harsh-weather months when staying inside is the best option anyway. Learn your tax skills by getting trained to be an IRS volunteer providing free tax help for qualifying taxpayers. Alternatively, you can enroll in one of the many tax preparer training programs available across the country.

LIBRARIAN ASSISTANT OR AIDE

You enjoy reading and assisting others. A library is an excellent place to work. Typical responsibilities include shelving books, sending out overdue notices, data entry, and assisting patrons with a variety of library requests. Working in the library provides a relaxing, air-conditioned environment with plenty of opportunities for learning.

GREETER

Put on a happy face, greet customers, and get paid. It's a good job for older workers who are unable or unwilling to perform physically demanding tasks in big-box stores, restaurants, and hotels. Of course, an outgoing personality is required to maintain a happy face for hours.

LEARN A NEW SKILL

"ANYONE WHO STOPS LEARNING IS OLD, WHETHER AT 20 OR 80.
ANYONE WHO KEEPS LEARNING STAYS YOUNG.
THE GREATEST THING IN LIFE IS TO KEEP YOUR MIND YOUNG."

-HENRY FORD-

Putting yourself out there to learn something new is fun and keeps the brain in good shape. Attending workshops and formal classes is one option; however, depending on what you want to learn, you could also look into free online videos that demonstrate the techniques you want to master. Think about learning how to:

BUILD A FIRE

Knowing how to build a fire and survive in the wilderness is an incredible skill to have. Not that you'll be going on a wilderness adventure anytime soon, but having the skills is an adventure in and of itself.

COOK A DIFFERENT TYPE OF CUISINE

Cooking is another enjoyable skill to learn. Whether you're a novice or an experienced chef, there's always something new to learn in the kitchen. Knowing how to cook makes life more enjoyable and delicious. Not just for yourself or your spouse, but for your family and friends as well.

CREATIVE WRITING

Discover the benefits of creative writing for senior health. Writing not only relieves stress but also improves mental dexterity!

DRAW A MANDALA

Mandalas are used spiritually by many different cultures around the world. Drawing a mandala is about much more than just drawing. The mandala's shape represents the universe, and drawing one is beneficial for self-discovery, healing, and is thought to be the purest form of self-expression. And once you've mastered the fundamentals of drawing a mandala, you can start creating your own unique mandalas by experimenting with different colors and designs. It's also a very mindful activity that can help you relax and unwind. So, whenever you're feeling stressed, draw a mandala.

DO THE MOONWALK

The moonwalk is one of the most well-known dance moves of all time. Those who are good at the moonwalk make it look so easy. However, you do not need to be a professional dancer to perform the moonwalk, so clear out your living room or bedroom and begin practicing.

FOLD TOWELS INTO ANIMALS

Have you taken a Carnival Cruise? If you have, you will understand what I mean. But if you haven't already, let me tell you about something cool. When housekeeping cleaned your cabin every day, they would leave an animal (folded towel) on your bed. Some of these animals were the most imaginative works of art. And this, too, is a simple new skill to learn today. Especially if you have a lot of guests staying with you. You can use folded towel art to surprise your grandchildren or guests.

DRIVE AN 18-WHEELER

While most truck drivers agree that driving an 18-wheeler isn't difficult, there is a learning curve to operating such a large vehicle. You'll need a lot more space to turn, back up, or change lanes, and you'll have much larger blind spots to compensate for.

GENEALOGY STUDY

It gives you a sense of identity. Discovering more about your ancestors, celebrating family traditions, embracing your culture, and understanding where you came from can open your eyes to how unique you are. It can also give your sense of self-worth and belonging a boost.

JUGGLE

Juggling is another enjoyable new skill to learn. Did you know it can also help you as a senior in a variety of ways? To begin, it is a low-impact exercise that strengthens your arms. On the other hand, juggling improves hand-eye coordination, balance, fine-motor skills, and relieves stress. This improves your health and happiness.

LEARN TO EAT WITH CHOPSTICKS

Have you ever traveled to an Asian country or restaurant and been astounded by how people ate with chopsticks? So, why not start learning how to eat with chopsticks today? Your new skills will impress some people the next time you eat at your favorite Thai restaurant.

LEARN YOGA

Yoga is a low-impact physical exercise that aims to bring mind and body into harmony. Meditation and yoga frequently go hand in hand. For more active seniors, yoga is a great mindfulness activity that can have the same effect as meditation.

LEARN YOUR PET A NEW TRICK

Do you have a dog or a cat? Then it's entertaining to teach them a new trick. You don't need to be a dog trainer or take a class to learn how to train your dog. There are numerous entertaining YouTube videos available that can teach you a variety of tricks.

MAKE AN ORIGAMI

Do you enjoy being inventive? Making an origami flower is a fun, creative skill you can learn today.

LEARN YOYO TRICKS

Return to your childhood, when yoyoing was still cool, and learn some new tricks.

MAKE LATTE ART

Do you enjoy drinking coffee? Learning how to make latte art is an enjoyable skill to acquire. You can surprise someone with heart-shaped coffee tomorrow.

NEW GARDENING TECHNIQUE

NEW ACTIVE PURSUITS LIKE GOLF, TENNIS, BILLIARDS, BOWLING, OR DANCING

PERFORM A MAGIC TRICK

Many magic tricks require hours or months of practice, but there are some that anyone can learn in a matter of minutes. This is an excellent skill for parties and social gatherings.

PAINT LIKE AN ARTIST

Painting is a skill that many people want to learn. So why not give it a shot? You never know unless you try, right?

PHOTO EDITING

PLAY A SONG ON THE PIANO

Do you have a piano at home, but you can't play it? So, dust it off because you can learn to play the piano today.

REPAIR A LEAKING SINK

Having the skills of a handyman can not only save you money, but it can also make your life easier, efficient, and increase the value of your home if done correctly. So, if you haven't already begun learning how to do basic home repairs, today is most likely a good day.

SOCIAL GAMES (FOR EXAMPLE, DOMINOES, BRIDGE, OR MAHJONG)

SCUBA DIVE

SOLVE A RUBIK'S CUBE

Solving a Rubik's cube does not have to involve aimlessly moving the pieces around for hours on end. You can solve a Rubik's cube quickly and easily if you know the formula or algorithm. It will undoubtedly impress many people.

SPEAK A NEW LANGUAGE

Many people's bucket lists include learning a new language. It's fun to know a few words in another language, but speaking and writing in a new language takes a lot of time, practice, and effort.

SPIRITUAL PRACTICES LIKE MEDITATION

Knowing how to meditate instantly makes your life more peaceful and calm. It's not a skill that you can learn once and then use for the rest of your life. If you want to have more inner peace throughout your day, week, month, and years ahead, you should practice it on a regular basis. You will improve as you practice, but each meditation session is an experience in and of itself. Sometimes it's more difficult than others. Accepting this is a necessary part of the mediation skill.

TAKE BETTER PHOTOS

Taking photographs is so simple these days. The quality of smartphone lenses improves year after year, but there is a lot more to taking better photos. Knowing how to adjust camera settings, finding the right perspective and composition, experimenting with lighting, and so on can help you go from taking average photos to taking amazing photos. Perhaps you'll take such beautiful photos that you want to use them as wall art.

VIDEO EDITING

You can learn video editing techniques to help you create better how-to videos, documentaries, travel stories, music videos, wedding films, commercials, and other types of videos.

WEB CODING

How can an older adult learn to code a website? There are several approaches to learning to code. Some online programs provide free courses, allowing individuals to learn at their own pace. For example, Codecademy. com is a free interactive website that teaches programming languages.

GET INVOLVED IN THE POLITICAL SCENE

"MANKIND WILL NEVER SEE AN END OF TROUBLE
UNTIL LOVERS OF WISDOM COME TO HOLD POLITICAL POWER,
OR THE HOLDERS OF POWER
BECOME LOVERS OF WISDOM."

-PLATO-

Do you consider yourself an activist? There is no better time than retirement to become more involved in issues affecting your city, state, or country as a whole.

BECOME A POLL WORKER

In general elections in the United States, older people make up a sizable proportion of poll workers and voters.

VOLUNTEER IN ELECTION CAMPAIGNS

If you find a candidate whose views you share, offer to help the campaign by knocking on doors and making phone calls on their behalf.

JOIN A GROUP

Whether you care about clean air and water or the rights of people with disabilities, you can join a group working on these and hundreds of other issues to make a difference and meet people who share your beliefs.

ORGANIZE A CANDIDATE FORUM

Invite candidates and local politicians to speak at a town hall, library, park district, senior center, or senior living community public meeting.

COLLECT SIGNATURES ON PETITIONS

The best way to grow a petition is to simply ask as many people as possible to sign it. You might be surprised at who is interested and wants to help you!

ATTEND A RALLY

Attend a candidate rally to become more informed and energized.

REACH OUT TO YOUR REPRESENTATIVES

Send letters, e-mails, and phone calls to your representatives to express your concerns or write an editorial for your local newspaper.

STAY INFORMED

Read and watch the news, converse with others, and participate in meetings, speeches, and debates.

VOTE!

Vote in person at the proper polling location, or vote early or absentee if you will be traveling or homebound due to health issues.

RUN FOR LOCAL OFFICE

Perhaps you've worked on political campaigns, volunteered for a community organization, or become a local issue advocate. Running for office can be a more rewarding way to effect change and serve your community. State and local offices, which are usually part-time, paid positions, can shape everything from health services and education to criminal justice.

Enjoy Events that Interest You

"Passion Is Energy. Feel The Power That Comes From Focusing On What Excites You."

-Oprah Winfrey-

Learn about the special events taking place in your community so that you can attend whatever appeals to you.

CONCERTS

We all go to concerts for various reasons: to see or meet our favorite band, to meet other fans in the crowd, to escape the stresses of life, and, ultimately, to have a good time.

THEATER SHOWS

The theater is a great place to explore new ideas while socializing with a group of friends.

SPORTS COMPETITIONS

Is there anything better than watching the world's best athletes compete on the biggest stages?

MONSTER TRUCK RALLIES

A great dirt track, massive trucks, and competition that is exciting and fun, everyone will really enjoy this sport!

FILM FESTIVALS

The festivals, which are sponsored by national or local governments, industry, service organizations, experimental film groups, or individual promoters, allow interested people to attend film screenings and meet to discuss current artistic developments in film.

GO TO SUMMER CAMP

"LOOK DEEP INTO NATURE, AND THEN
YOU WILL UNDERSTAND EVERYTHING BETTER."

-ALBERT EINSTEIN-

A growing number of specialized camps offer canoeing, ziplining, archery, river rafting, ropes courses, climbing walls, and campfires to older adults. Adapted activities are available for those who have physical limitations. Most camps offer comfortable lodges, often in air-conditioned accommodations with private bathrooms, so you won't be roughing it like you did when you were younger. Couples are permitted to bunk together in some camps, while male and female campers are separated in others. For a week-long stay that includes all meals and activities, prices range from around $500 to more than $1,400. Here are a few options to consider:

CAMP CHIEF OURAY

For kids ages 50 and up. Why should the kids have all the fun?! Get away and enjoy time in the mountains with campers who are 50 years young and above. Get ready for fun and new friends as this camp is designed with your special interests and abilities in mind. The choice is yours, be as active or as relaxed as you like in our fun and supportive environment.

CITY OF SACRAMENTO SENIOR SUMMER CAMP

Spend a week in summer at Camp Sacramento, enjoying the beauty of the majestic Sierras. The City of Sacramento's 50+ Wellness Program hosts affordable mini vacations at Camp Sacramento in the Eldorado National Forest along Highway 50, just 18 miles west of Lake Tahoe. At an elevation of 6,500 feet, with the tall pines, clear blue sky, and meandering river, Camp Sacramento provides a scenic setting that offers a wonderful way to relax in the mountains.

SUMMER CAMP WITH YOUR FAMILY IN THE OZARKS

Take your family to summer camp in the Ozark foothills. On an amazing adventure, go horseback riding, float down the river, and fly through the forest on an Alpine Swing (open to seniors along with their adult children and grandchildren over age 10).

CAMP ISABELLA FREEDMAN

Head to the Berkshires to enjoy 400 acres of summer-filled fun geared towards adults 55 and older. Spend a week boating on the lake, swimming in the pool, exploring the nature trails, or attending classes. We'll have arts and crafts, dance and movement, memorable films, talent shows, camp-fires, and lakeside happy hours.

CAMP GETAWAY

Just 90 short miles from NYC in Kent, Connecticut, sits an old-school summer camp just for adults. Camp Getaway allows you to reconnect with your inner child. Leave your life behind and travel to a place where the only schedule you follow is one filled with adventure after breakfast and evening parties.

CAMP NO COUNSELOR'S LOS ANGELES

Spend a weekend at a social summer camp; you'll find a coupling of tra-ditional daytime activities (ropes courses, kayaking, and more) and nightly socials complete with foam parties, live music, and more.

NEEDLEPOINT CAMP

Stitching is making a comeback as one of the most popular hobbies, and the Needlepoint Retreats will help you hone your skills while socializing with other like-minded individuals.

SPACE CAMP

Always wanted to be an astronaut? The Adult Space Camp in Huntsville, Alabama, is quite literally out of this world. During the five-night weekend—offered once per month from May through September—you'll learn what it takes to be an astronaut with hands-on experience navigating interactive space missions.

GRILLING CAMP

Yes, you read that right. At Meat Camp, guests stay in luxury safari platform tents on the property of Belcampo Farms in Northern California. Here they learn to cut, grill, serve, and sauce meat, mix up farm cocktails, and enjoy nightly fireside chats.

UPSCALE SUMMER CAMP

Wisconsin's Camp Halcyon lives up to its name, which means "a period of time that was idyllically happy and peaceful." Surrounded by gorgeous scenery, camp-goers can choose from a range of traditional pastimes or indulge in wine tastings, yoga on the beach, and fine food.

DUDE RANCH CAMP

Six times each year (twice in May, once in June, twice in August, and once in September), Black Mountain Ranch, nestled in the mountains of McCoy, Colorado, offers a more intimate experience for adults only. The all-inclusive stay includes unlimited horseback rides, whitewater rafting down the Colorado River, shooting, fishing, and swimming, paired with gourmet meals and live music.

EMPOWERMENT CAMP

Tucked in Ojai, California, Campowerment is a women-only summer camp where campers are encouraged to shed all titles (from CEO to mom) and connect with the environment, themselves, and the other women in attendance.

BAND CAMP

In the heart of central Maine sits a band camp for adults. New England Adult Music Camp is a place where musicians of all levels come together to hone skills, try new instruments, and enjoy the beautiful lakeside setting.

GOLF CAMP

The Lake Placid Resort & Spa golf camp is a three-day school (dates flexible) in Lake Placid, New York, where players are coached through all facets of the game—from full swing to putting—by a top team of LPGA and PGA instructors.

VIRTUAL HAPPINESS CAMP

Not quite ready to hop on a plane or share a cabin with others? The Virtual Happiness Retreat allows you to get a bit of the camp experience without ever leaving your home. Throughout the course of two days, you'll "explore" Tuscany through cooking classes and wine tastings, plus participate in mindfulness activities, like yoga and meditation, to leave you feeling just as rejuvenated as you might have you taken a true vacation. Dates are flexible, too. Watch whenever you want for up to six months from the date of purchase.

EXPLORE YOUR FAMILY HISTORY

"FAMILIES ARE LIKE BRANCHES ON A TREE.
WE GROW IN DIFFERENT DIRECTIONS
YET OUR ROOTS REMAIN AS ONE.."

-UNKNOWN-

After retirement, many people become more interested in their family histories and, with more free time, begin researching their ancestors. They become keepers of family history, passing it down to their children and grandchildren as they discover information to fill gaps in their family trees. So, delve into your roots and discover where you came from. This could involve:

SORTING OLD FAMILY PHOTOS

It is critical that you protect these family memories by organizing and storing your old family photos. Photographs and other types of media have an expiration date; if not properly stored, they deteriorate over time.

SCAN OLD FAMILY PHOTOS

Take advantage of this opportunity not only to scan your photos but also to organize them and identify people, events, and locations. Look for mobile scanning apps if you don't already have a scanner but have a cell phone with a camera. Some will not only scan your photo, but will also upload it to a cloud storage service. Many provide photo editing and tagging tools.

OLD STORIES

Gather a collection of stories passed down through the generations. Stories are what bring our family trees and all of our genealogy work to life! The stories of our forefathers' lives can come to us from a variety of sources. Many come from our elders and other members of our extended family, often aunts, uncles, and cousins who enjoy sharing a wide range of memories. Old newspapers are another excellent source of information about our forefathers.

TRACK DOWN DETAILS ABOUT YOUR ANCESTORS

Historical and government records can assist you in tracing your ancestors. Use these free resources to conduct family tree research and construction. The National Archives and Records Administration has a collection of genealogy resources.

BUILD A FAMILY TREE

You can use websites like Ancestry and MyHeritage, but a paid subscription is required to access the complete range of resources (prices range from $80 to $200 per year). Or check out Family History Daily's list of free genealogy resources for each state.

FIND GRANDPARENTS IN CENSUS RECORDS

Perhaps you "know" they lived in a specific location but can't find them. If you haven't already, now is the time to experiment with deep search techniques such as searching with wildcards, searching only by first name or surname, searching by combinations of family members, or searching for names that sound similar. Consider going through enumeration districts or counties page by page. Alternatively, take the opposite approach and search more broadly.

START A FAMILY HISTORY BOOK OR SCRAPBOOK

Uploading photos and arranging them with text is simple with online services like Snapfish, Shutterfly, and Mixbook. Begin by focusing on a small family group or an individual, or consider a theme or event, such as holidays or family vacations.

TAKE A DNA TEST

Include DNA evidence in your documentary research, or consider transferring your test results to a different company to find new matches and research avenues.

COOK A DISH FROM AN ANCESTRAL LAND

Teach your children a family recipe, or look up traditional menus from an ancestor's home country. Cookbooks and other resources about these traditions from around the world may be available in your library's ebook collection.

LEARN THE LANGUAGE OF YOUR ANCESTORS

Duolingo and Memrise are two free language learning apps and websites. Some public libraries also offer language-learning programs to cardholders.

RECORD YOUR OWN LIFE STORY

Genealogists frequently overlook their own personal histories. Aside from documenting your own reactions to living through this historical period, consider writing about your childhood, school days, or life as a young adult. What about your parents, grandparents, and other family members do you recall?

DIVE INTO ONLINE COURT RECORDS

Now is the time to look through those old ledgers for ancestors. Learn more about the various record types, why they were created, and who created them, and look for a mention of your family in them. Although many have been digitized, they are not always indexed and may necessitate a lengthy manual search.

RECORD FAMILY TRADITIONS

We frequently consider memorable holiday customs, but what else does the family "always" do, make, or say? In August, do you go to the lake? Do all of the family's infants wear the same christening gown? When and why did that tradition begin? What is the significance to your family?

LEARN ABOUT AN ANCESTOR'S OCCUPATION

Once you've learned about that occupation, look for record collections that may contain additional information. Don't overlook local and state libraries, archives, and societies, which may have very specific information about an ancestor's employer or line of work.

REACH OUT TO DNA MATCHES

You never know what you might learn by contacting recently added DNA matches or those more distant matches you haven't prioritized yet.

JOIN A GENEALOGY FACEBOOK GROUP

There are Facebook discussion groups for almost every genealogical interest, location, and skill level, making it an excellent way to stay social while also expanding your genealogical knowledge.

MAP YOUR ANCESTORS

Follow migration and learn more about each stop along the way, as well as how your ancestors may have made the journey. And where exactly is that ancestral hometown? You might even be able to take a virtual tour of the location using Google Street View!

UPLOAD PICTURES TO YOUR ONLINE FAMILY TREE

This gives you another method of backup storage, but it can also entice more cousins when they come across an image of a familiar face while searching.

BE A VIRTUAL VOLUNTEER

Contribute to other online projects by indexing or transcribing records. Although FamilySearch's indexing program is probably the most well-known, other libraries, archives, and organizations also have volunteer projects. ConferenceKeeper has a good selection to choose from. Don't forget to contact your local or state society!

CONCLUSION

"CHALLENGES ARE GIFTS THAT FORCE US TO SEARCH FOR
A NEW CENTER OF GRAVITY. DON'T FIGHT THEM.
JUST FIND A NEW WAY TO STAND."

-OPRAH WINFREY-

"I don't know what I'd do, I'd just end up being bored," is a common objection to retirement that I frequently hear.

There is no doubt that retirement requires some adjusting and planning (not just financially), but how can you be bored when there are so many things to do: experiences to have, expertise to share, skills to learn, time to give, and knowledge to acquire?

You found a list of so many different things in this book.

Some require money, while others do not.

Some require travel, while others can be done from home.

Some are selfish, while others are charitable.

However, regardless of gender, background, ability, or financial means, there is something for everyone.

Imagine the Possibilities…

Retirement is the most enjoyable and relaxing time in many people's lives. You have the freedom to engage in a variety of activities that keep you interested and engaged. So consider your goals and dreams, and start making them a reality!

MY NOTES

My Notes